FAITH

"WHEN THE SON OF MAN COMES,
WILL HE FIND FAITH ON THE EARTH?"
—JESUS (LUKE 18:8)

JAY R. ASHBAUCHER

innovo
PUBLISHING

Published by Innovo Publishing, LLC
www.innovopublishing.com
1-888-546-2111

innovo
PUBLISHING

Providing Full-Service Publishing Services for Christian Authors, Artists & Ministries:
Books, eBooks, Audiobooks, Music, Film & Courses

FAITH
Upload Your Faith Series (Book 2)

Scripture taken from the New American Standard Bible® Copyright © 1960,
1962, 1963, 1968, 1971, 1972, 1973, 1975, 1977, 1995 by The Lockman
Foundation. Used by permission.

The Holy Bible: International Standard Version. Release 2.0, Build 2015.02.09.
Copyright © 1995-2014 by ISV Foundation. ALL RIGHTS RESERVED
INTERNATIONALLY. Used by permission of Davidson Press, LLC.

Library of Congress Control Number: 2019909219
ISBN: 978-1-61314-487-9

Cover Design & Interior Layout: Innovo Publishing, LLC

Printed in the United States of America
U.S. Printing History
First Edition: 2019

CONTENTS

ACKNOWLEDGING GRATITUDE

To the God of all faith and hope, for his life-giving Word and his Spirit's guidance in this writing.

To my wife, Connie, for suggestions, patience with me through many disappearings to work on the project, and encouraging support.

To my brother, Reid, for suggestions and technical support.

To the men of my Montana small group who contributed much to my walk with Christ and who continue to influence my thinking and goals.

To my readers, for motivation to finish another book of teachings from God's Word.

To Trinity Evangelical Divinity School, for giving me a Christian worldview, respect for others' views, and valued training in what it means to be entrusted with the truths of the Bible and the gospel of Jesus (1 Thessalonians 2:4).

To Innovo Publishing and Rachael Carrington, my editor, for much-needed wisdom and help along the way.

INTRODUCTION AND PREFACE

This is the second in a series of three books. The first book, titled *The Power of Life-Giving Hope in Troublesome Times*, deals with the meaning and value of hope. The second book explores the subject of faith. The third book will examine the subject of God's love and its contribution to human love. These three subjects, faith, hope, and love, make up the three great aims and practices in the life of a Christian (1 Corinthians 13:13).

The goal of this book is to help readers learn about faith and grow in faith, so that faith is an ever-present help in daily life and in difficult times. This book will define faith, help you identify the weaknesses or strengths of *your* faith, reveal the source of faith, answer questions about faith, and help you know how to use faith to overcome character defects, as well as stressful, trying times.

Faith-killers are things that prevent a confident faith. They include fear, worry, and anxiety. Other faith-killers may include not enough knowledge to know if the object you believe in can be trusted, having no guaranteed hope, problems with unanswered prayers, disturbing doubts, or negative past experiences that make trusting difficult. Faith overcomes these objects, enabling us to please God, have confidence in him, and overcome an evil world that depresses us and destroys our lives.

Faith is not always easy, but when confidently exercised, it produces inner quietness and peace. In addition, if the object of your faith is ultimately trustworthy, then no matter what, it results in the hope that everything will be all right. Faith is a part of everyone's life, but not everyone has the kind of faith that overcomes what the world throws at him or her. Although God's blessings in our lives are wonderful, God does not bless his people with a pain-free life. In fact, in a fallen world like ours, it seems God must necessarily allow trials of all kinds as a way to deepen our faith. Without trials we would not grow to meet God's definition of maturity, which is to achieve Christlikeness (Romans 8:29; Galatians 4:19) and to be holy as God is holy (Leviticus 11:45; 19:2; Matthew 5:48; 1 Peter 1:14-16).

Faith does not allow itself to be attached to this world. It believes in something greater. It believes in the hope of God that allows us "to live securely and be at ease from the dread of evil" (Proverbs 1:32-33). Faith believes in the truth that God has revealed. Without faith we are bound for self-destruction and death. This was typified by the unbelieving Israelites whom God wanted to save, who had God's good news spoken to them, but who died in the wilderness. "The word they heard did not profit them, because it was not united by faith" (Hebrews 4:1-2).

Faith is not without its difficulties. Some things are hard to believe. We have doubts and questions. Whenever I contemplate the object of my faith, mostly the content of the Bible, I seem to end up with more questions than answers. Some questions have to do with curiosity and wanting to know the exact meaning of what I read. Other questions are threatening, disturbing, and bothersome to my faith because they seemingly challenge what I believe or want to believe. Some questions are disturbing questions about how I am doing, or not doing, at living my faith.

How we handle these questions has much to do with how we experience faith. Do we give up, or do we doubt our faith until we can satisfactorily answer certain questions? Are we interested enough to search for the answers, knowing our faith is strengthened with increased understanding? It helps to bolster our faith when we know more about it. Reasoning through difficulties is a part of helping to solidify our faith, although it must be recognized that there is much mystery to be accepted. Knowing more about our faith also enables us to help others who are struggling with their faith due to doubts or fears. We all have questions, but the most important question is not what we believe to be true, as if you and I determine truth. Rather, the most important question is this: What is it that is true that I need to believe?

Faith and prayer are closely related. I placed prayer last in this book because I want prayer to be the last thing that sticks in your mind as the most important thing you can do for increasing your faith. Prayer is vitally connected with faith, and I want readers to know better how to engage God in prayer and to think about how important it is to put it first in their lives. When Jesus taught us to pray, the first thing he taught was to begin with acknowledging God's name, Father, asking that his name be honored and his will be done. The conclusion of chapter ten will explain why prayer is such an important part of our faith.

My prayer is that this book will help people better understand faith, see how faith relates to all areas of life, know how to use faith to overcome problems, and through faith, experience God and be blessed by him. Chapters on how faith helps one overcome addictions and how it helps one with a positive self-identity will help lead readers out of deep personal issues that are defeating them. Faith is extremely important, for the Bible says that without faith, it is impossible to please God, and that it's our faith that enables us to overcome the world (Hebrews 11:6; 1 John 5:4).

From where does faith come? The Apostle Paul said, "Faith comes from hearing, and hearing by the word of Christ" (Romans 10:17). I take this to mean that we must hear something before we can believe it, and the best thing to believe is a word from God himself, especially his Word concerning Christ. This book offers a lot to be heard, and it offers plenty of words from God. I pray the words of this book and the words of God's book will spark your faith—no, rather that these words will set your faith on fire, so that you will see and experience God's presence and goodness at work in your life as never before.

CHAPTER 1

WHAT IS FAITH?

One definition of faith is this: "Faith is having complete trust, reliance, or confidence in someone or something to provide what is needed or desired."[1] Everybody has faith in someone or something. In fact, life cannot be functional and happily lived without faith. The farmer, for instance, needs to plant a crop to make a living. He knows the crop may dry up for lack of rain, or fail from other kinds of disasters like hail, diseases, or bugs. The risks involved could keep him from planting; nevertheless, he plants and takes care of his crop with faith that all will work out. Faith is how we live because there is rarely, if ever, 100 percent certainty about anything. Because we are all limited in knowledge, faith closes the gap between certainty and uncertainty, enabling us to do the daily things that need doing.

Faith is often as easy as breathing; we do not have to think about it. Here are examples of ways we daily exercise faith with little or no thought: When we drive a car, we do not hesitate even though it could break down and leave us stranded. We trust the car. When I purchase food at the store or farmer's market, I don't refuse to eat it for fear of impurities. I trust the food source. When a friend tells me they will meet me at a certain time and place, I have no guarantee until they show up, but I go to the place of meeting because I trust their word.

---

1. This definition is simply a starter to get us thinking. I put it together based on knowledge I've gained from English dictionaries, theological dictionaries, and from reading the Bible. There are other definitions of faith that you will encounter in this chapter and book.

We once had a dinner guest who sat down with us to enjoy a meal and family conversation. Suddenly the front leg of his chair broke, and he had to regain his balance to prevent possible embarrassment or injury. Can you imagine going through life, having to check everything out to make sure it was safe before you did anything? Our guest's experience could cause him never to trust a chair again, but it is quite likely that by now he is back to chair sitting without worrying if the chair will fail him. It is easy to have faith in things that have a long-standing record of proving trustworthy. Interestingly, we have a responsibility to work at maintaining some of the objects of our faith, otherwise the objects become untrustworthy.

Faith, however, is not always easy to exercise. Some faith involves a higher degree of risk, and higher risk elevates worry and fear. If people allow worries and fears to control them, they will not risk stepping out in faith. For example, some will not fly in airplanes, fearing a crash. Others will not invest in stock markets for fear of losing their savings. Some people do not trust doctors, so they resist going to them, even if it means facing a life-threatening health problem. Some go through their entire house when they return home late at night to make sure no one is lurking in the shadows. Lacking 100 percent certainty can allow fear, worry, anxiety, or doubts to control us and limit a functional and happy life. Lacking knowledge in the trustworthiness of an object or person makes faith more difficult.

Sometimes, to achieve what needs doing, we must choose, after much struggle, to risk stepping out and trusting the object of our faith. During a backpacking trip in the mountains, I came to a wide part in a river. I was weary after a long day of hiking with a heavy pack on my back, and now I had to cross the river on logs. I started to cross, but sudden fear of falling overcame me and I froze in the middle. I could not take another step. I had lost faith in myself and needed to regain confidence that I could make it to the other side. It took a few minutes of mental struggle to regain belief that I could do this. At times like that, we want to safely remain where we are. It doesn't feel like faith is easy, but without faith, we don't take important steps forward. Without faith, I might still be on the log, or floundering in the water. Life cannot be functional and happily lived without exercising faith.

In Christianity, faith is something we frequently hear people refer to when they are struggling to get through rough times. When people share with us the hard thing they are going through, our heart goes out to them, and we wonder how they can endure it. Often, a concerned person will ask them how they are managing to get through it, and the person will respond by saying, "If it wasn't for my faith, I don't think I could make it." Or, "I could never make it without God. I don't know how people without faith do it." What do Christians mean when they say this? How and why is their faith helping them? A more pointed question than, "How are you managing to get through it?" might be, "In what ways is your faith helping you?"

THE SOURCE OF FAITH

People choose many different things to believe in to help them get through life. Some people put faith in reason. Some put faith in science. Some put faith in religion. Some put faith in government and politics. Some have faith in human goodness. Some believe in a particular philosophy or ethical truth to guide their lives. Some, finding others untrustworthy, will only trust themselves. The objects we believe in are numerous. There is no doubt we have some degree of faith in all of the above, but the big question is this: Is there an object of faith, among life's immense diversity and choices, that will make my life as functional and happily lived as possible? It is a huge task, and worth the effort, to search for the most worthy object of faith. Our faith best rewards us when the object we believe in proves able to make our life the best it can be. And how fortunate we are, if in our seeking the most worthy object, that object unexpectedly finds us (Luke 15:4-6; 19:10).

What determines or drives our search for a worthy object to believe in? Is there not some kind of thirst or hunger within each of us for something that meets our deepest need (John 7:37)? Is it hunger for answers to nagging questions, or for love and belonging, or for emotional health? Do we hunger for freedom from evils that

13

terrorize us, or for something that will help us become a better person? Do we hunger to find the greatest purpose and meaning in life? Do we hunger for things like power or riches or popularity? We all have hungers that drive us to find what will satisfy us. To be honest, most of our hungers are self-centered, which is not necessarily wrong, but it brings up a primary question: *Am I hungering for the right things?* And if so, *Will whatever I am trusting to satisfy my hunger deliver what it promises?*

If any objects of our faith prove inadequate, as they often do, we look for new ones. Our search goes on until we settle on whatever proves to be the most rewarding object, or objects, to believe in. This book will present a great object of faith, one that will give the utmost results. But in this chapter, our focus is to define the word *faith*.

THREE COMPONENTS DEFINE FAITH

First, faith always has *an object*. We believe in something, and our faith counts on that something being real and trustworthy. The object must produce the expectations it promises, or it will result in disappointing or dangerous outcomes. Faith that a plane will get us to our desired destination lets us down if the plane fails to make it. Faith that the person we marry will give us companionship and happiness fails if the relationship becomes problematic. Faith that Jesus's body raised from the dead, guaranteeing us a resurrection like his, does no good if his resurrection is not a true and reliable fact. The Apostle Paul admits that if Christ is not raised from the dead, then our faith is worthless (1 Corinthians 15:12-20).

Second, faith not only involves an object; faith requires our *assent or agreement* that the object is real and trustworthy. For example, if we take an elevator in a multi-storied building, or cross a bridge high over a river, or believe we will go out of existence after we die, or believe in the resurrection of our bodies, we must agree that these objects we believe in will do what they are promising to do. We must accept the object of our faith as true and reliable if we are to risk believing in it.

Some need more answers than others do to questions like, "Is it true?" and "How do I know?" They cannot give their *assent or agreement* without answers to their questions or doubts. Although "faith alone" could result in an object that gives a person all it promises, for many or most, faith is not a blind leap. They need reasons to help persuade them to believe that the object of their trust will not fail them. Before believing, many people need to check things out.

I remember a story Francis Schaeffer posed about a man caught in a blinding, life-threatening, icy fog during his climb up a mountain. Unable to go forward or backward, he was stuck on the edge of a cliff, and survival seemed hopeless. To avoid freezing to death, he could imagine there existed a ledge ten feet beneath him that he could drop down onto and find protection during the night. Yet how foolish to take a leap of blind faith and risk falling to his death. But what if a man from across the way, who had been watching him, and who knew the mountain, yelled to him that if he would let himself drop over the edge, he would land on a ledge and be safe until rescue. After further conversation with the man, and based on acceptable reasons, he could more easily agree that his object of faith is worth trusting.[2] Faith often involves adequate reasons before believing. We want to be reasonably sure that what we believe in can deliver what it promises. Even after believing, questions or doubts may arise, and further adequate reasons can strengthen a person's faith.

Third, faith requires *commitment*—the surrender of our life to what, or who, we believe in. We can see and believe in a boat and, based on reason or experience, acknowledge that the boat is real and can get us across a lake, but unless we get into the boat, commit our lives into its care, and let it take us there, we will not get to our desired destination. Faith means committing our life into the care of the object of our faith. Faith is subjective. It is something we exercise, something we do.

DEFINING THE OBJECT OF CHRISTIAN FAITH

All religions and human ideologies have a body of knowledge that forms the content of their faith. The Bible uses two words, *the faith*, meaning the body of knowledge that makes up the content, or

2. Francis A. Schaeffer, *He is There and He is Not Silent* (Wheaton, IL: Tyndale House, 1972) 99–100.

object, of the Christian faith. Acts 6:7 says that the Word of God kept on spreading, and many were becoming obedient to *the faith*. Later on in Acts we read that the believers were encouraged to continue in *the faith* (Acts 14:21-22). What made up *the faith* in the context of these verses in Acts is the gospel, which means the good news about who Jesus Christ is and what he did and said. This includes information about him, both before and after his birth (Luke 24:44-48). When the Apostle Paul was converted, it was said about him that "he who once persecuted [the Christians] is now preaching *the faith* which he once tried to destroy" (Galatians 1:23, emphasis added). In Jude 1:3 we read that believers are to "contend earnestly for *the faith* which was once for all handed down to the saints" (emphasis added). Even though there is a lot of content that makes up *the faith*, the primary object of faith for the Christian is Jesus Christ. We are to entrust our lives to a person. He claimed to be the way, the truth, and the life for anyone who would put their faith in him (John 14:6, 11). The content of Christian faith, including the good news about Jesus, includes God's revealed truths found in both the Old and New Testaments of the Bible. We could also extend *the faith* to include any knowledge of God we learn from observing his created universe (Romans 1:20).

Here are two biblical examples illustrating the three components of faith: (1) When the Israelites had to cross the Jordan River to enter their Promised Land, God told the priests to step into the water, and the waters would stop flowing, allowing them to cross. To experience their promised new life, they must agree to believe in God, believe what he said, and then commit their lives to act by stepping into the river (Joshua 3:9-17). When they took that step, the object of their faith proved trustworthy. (2) Thomas, a disciple of Jesus, demonstrated these three aspects of faith when he would not believe the other disciples' word that Jesus arose from the dead. Jesus appeared and showed Thomas his crucifixion wounds. Thomas now had sufficient reason to believe that Jesus was alive and was truly Lord and God (John 20:24-29). So convinced was he of the quality of life offered by such an object, and of the reality and trustworthiness of this object of faith, that he committed his life to following Christ, no matter what the cost. Sources say he suffered martyrdom in India for the cause of Christ. The object of his faith was the risen Lord. Our faith, although we do not now see Christ, is based on the witness of those who did. Jesus said, "Blessed are they who did not see, and yet believed" (John 20:29). Faith is subjective (something we do) but requires an objective element (what we believe).

CONCLUDING THOUGHTS

Faith involves three things: an *object* to believe in, *believing* the object is trustworthy, and the *commitment*, meaning the surrender of our lives, to that object. Faith willingly makes a commitment because we have good reason to believe that the object of our faith will fulfill what it promises. Is there any object that will *never* fail us (Deuteronomy 31:6-8; Joshua 21:45; Hebrews 13:5-6; 1 John 4:16)? What the Bible refers to as *the faith*, properly understood, promises to be such an object (John 11:25-26; 1 Corinthians 6:14; 2 Timothy 1:8-14). When we act and take whatever steps God tells us to take, that object of faith ultimately proves trustworthy.

When we read Hebrews 11:1 and think about the examples of faith in that chapter of the Bible, we see that faith is the substance or assurance of what we hope for, and the evidence or conviction of things not yet seen. This definition of faith is why some believe we do not need reasons to believe in God and in the truths of the Bible. They say we don't need reasons in order to believe; rather, if we believe, we will know. Faith itself knows that the things we believe in and hope for will one day become reality. The object of faith in this verse is the things we hope for/things yet unseen/the expected promises of God that we long for and patiently wait to experience. Faith believes God exists and will reward those who sincerely seek him (11:6). As seen in Hebrews 11, our faith may not always get us what we want, when we want it (11:13-16, 32-40). However, by putting our faith in the God who reveals himself in the scriptures, we know that no matter how things look to us, faith knows that God is there for us and will bring to pass the things he has promised. Nothing *this world* offers can fully guarantee to give humans what they need most.

Some individuals believe that we humans can determine our own truth, reality, and ultimate good. In this case, the object of faith is ourselves. However, most humans realize their own limitations. That explains why worldwide religions exist. Because worry and fear are ongoing realities in this world, people depend on a source of more power and help beyond anything we or this world can offer. Prayer and faith is the way humans connect with their religious source. Christians look to a person, the God and Christ revealed in the Bible, as the only savior who guarantees the fulfillment of all that is ultimately good (Acts 4:12). The Apostle Paul said, "It is no longer I who live, but Christ lives in me, and the life which I now live in the flesh, I live by faith in the Son of God, who loved me and gave himself up for me" (Galatians 2:20). Life is most functional and happily lived when one is exercising faith in God and Christ Jesus. Even in the worst of times, our faith is that which provides us with a certain God-given hope that calms us and sees us through (Hebrews 11:1; Psalm 56:3-4). I heard someone once define faith as that something deep inside of us, which we hang onto until help comes.

CHAPTER 2

WHY GOD WROTE A BOOK

THE OVERALL REASON GOD WROTE A BOOK

God wrote to tell us his story. His story provides the primary content of Christian faith. That story, God's salvation story, is what the Bible is all about. It is the greatest story ever told, the true story of humankind and earth's history from its beginning in Genesis to its ending in Revelation. Most often, when we read chapter by chapter, we get only bits and pieces of the story; but to become truly excited about it, we need to see the whole story. As God reveals himself to us and we come to believe in him, we will come to see how we fit in, to understand our part in his story. Once we envision God's story and *experience* our part in it, we can't help but tell it to others. We tell it with our life and with our words. The more we tell it, the more excited, hopeful, and joy-filled we become. We become excited and joy-filled because we know who God is, who we are, why we are here, where we are going, and how to get there. When we understand, have faith in, and experience God's story, things like love, peace, joy, oneness, hope, and all that is good in us will increase, while things like fear, anxiety, sadness, grief, isolation, hopelessness, and all that is bad in us will decrease.

To give you a brief overview of God's story, I will begin by stating five basic points that tell the story. I will then give a very short version of the story by adding a little more detail to each point. The Bible, of course, gives us the complete version of the story, from which we will never run out of new things to learn. Following these brief overviews of God's story, I shall survey some of the specific reasons found in the Bible for why God wrote a book. Perhaps people would be more motivated to read the Bible if they knew his story and his reasons for writing it.

FIVE BASIC STATEMENTS THAT TELL GOD'S STORY

Following are five basic statements that tell God's story:

1. God created the world and everything in it. All was good.

2. God's good world has fallen into evil and ruin.

3. The key to a restored world is God's promised savior.

4. In cooperation with people of faith, God works his plan to restore his world to goodness.

5. Through Christ, God creates a new and evil-free world.

A BRIEF EXPANSION OF THE FIVE BASIC STATEMENTS

1. There exists a one and only true and eternal God, a triune God, who created the world and everything in it. All that he made was good, for God is good and there is no evil in him. He created the earth to be the home for humans, with many hidden and marvelous things to discover, use, and enjoy. God created the heavens and the earth as a perfect environment for our well-being. Then, God created us humans in his image. Being in his image means that we display in our thoughts and behaviors the qualities of what God is like, including love and a free will to make choices. At the beginning, humans often met with God and enjoyed a close relationship with him.

2. God's good world has fallen into evil and ruin. God knew there was such a thing as evil that had potential to become real, and if such a thing were permitted to enter the world, it would ruin God's perfectly good world. God must have thought the choice between good and evil was necessary for humans with free will to have, so by making what he called *the tree of the knowledge of good and evil,* he set up the potential for evil to enter the world. God warned the people he created that if they allowed evil to enter by eating the fruit of that tree, they would die.

A creature, made by God, became evil and came to the first man and woman to try to get them to choose evil. Unfortunately, the first humans chose to listen to the tempter rather than to the warnings of God, and the curses of evil entered their lives and environment. They soon learned that to die meant they would lose the kind of life God had given them. Their relationships with God, each other, and the earth would be damaged and cursed. Death meant dying little by little with each thing they chose to do wrong. This progressing death, barring premature death, would end in aging and lifeless bodies. Ultimately, however, death would mean that if anyone chose not to come back to God as their life-giver, God would honor their choice to remain separate from him and his new earth and world.

Consider the problem we all face. How can our loving and holy Creator save us from the evils we have chosen to let into our lives and world? Infected and enslaved by the evils within us, our evil thoughts and actions are destroying us. We are guilty for choosing to ignore God's warnings, and he is bound by his holiness and justice to declare us unfit to enter his world of perfect righteousness. Therefore, we remain under the sentence of death and are without any hope of saving ourselves. God must devise a plan that allows his justice to be satisfied so that his love and mercy can forgive, save, and free us from evil.

3. The key to a restored people and world is a promised savior, who later in the story is called Messiah and Christ.

Knowing evil would happen to his creation, God, even before Creation, devised a plan to send a savior to rid his world of evil and restore it to goodness. Throughout the story, from the beginning to the end, God promises to send a savior. This promise is like a thread woven throughout the entire story, tying together its pieces and making all of human history one continuous story. The savior would be born into the world through a direct line of believing descendants chosen by God. That a Messianic line of descendants exists is demonstrated by genealogical records—for example, those in Luke 3:23-38 and Matthew 1:1-16. The success of God's plan for a savior to be born into his world requires preserving that line of descendants. Following the savior's entrance into the world, he would have to be endowed with God's character, will, power, wisdom, and blessing to fulfill what God needs to do to redeem his world, do away with evil, and restore his world to newness and goodness.

4. In cooperation with people of faith, God works his plan to restore his world to goodness. God's story, covering both Old and New Testaments, stretches over thousands of years. Early on in the story, as stated in point three above, God promises a savior (Genesis 3:15; 12:1-3; 13:14-16; 15:1-6, 18; 17:15-19; 22:1-18; Galatians 3:16). Up until the events surrounding the savior's birth, God must, at certain times, act to protect and preserve the line of descendants through which that Messiah will be born. The people who form this line of descendants are believers in what God says, and they have faith to trust and obey God's Word. Whenever that Messianic line is threatened, God intervenes in history to save his people and preserve his plan for the Christ to be born. He may do so by judging enemies who are trying to destroy his plan (Exodus 14:30-31), performing some kind of miracle to ensure its success, or influencing a person's heart or history's circumstances so those people and circumstances will favor God's people and plan (e.g., Ezra 1:1-4; Nehemiah 2:1-6; book of Esther; Matthew 2:13-20).

You may notice that many truths about the savior are given throughout the Old Testament part of the story—either by "pictures" of him being portrayed through people's experiences with God or by prophecies that include statements about the coming Messiah. When the savior comes, people will recognize him by how he fulfills those "illustrative pictures" and prophecies. (For example, see Genesis 22:1-18; Exodus 12:3-13; Psalm 22:1, 16-18; Micah 5:2. Compare Isaiah 61:1 and Luke 4:16-21 with Luke 7:18-23.)

After the promised savior's birth, the New Testament reveals all that must happen leading up to the end of God's *saving his world* story. The big event that makes possible God's salvation of the world is Jesus's death on a cross, his burial, and his bodily resurrection. God has always had people who believe in him and he expects his believing people to live and be witness to his events in such a way as to help others come to know the God who loves and saves. When Israel, the people through whom the savior came, fails to recognize God's plan in Christ Jesus, God forms another people, his church, to represent him. Christ returns to his Father in heaven, and God continues his saving work through his people, until Christ Jesus comes again to fulfill all promises made to his people, Jew and Gentile, and to restore all things.

God reveals himself in many ways and at various times throughout his story (Hebrews 1:1-2) so that believers and unbelievers can come to know the God who exists. God doesn't care only for his faithful believing ones; he cares about the people who do not believe. He does not want any to die but for all people to repent of their wrongs and believe in him (Ezekiel 18:32). Even though he judges the wicked who oppose his plan, including his own people who turn away from him, his judgments are just and not without warning and patience. God gives time and opportunity for people to repent and join with him.

As you read the biblical story, you will notice that as times and cultures change, the main theme, even up to the days in which we live, is always the same: the battle between good and evil. People's choices, good or bad, are clearly seen throughout the story. Yet through human imperfections, and in spite of poor choices, God remains faithful to keep his promise to save the world through his Christ.

5. The end of God's story is the hope of all who believe. In the end, through Christ's return to earth, God creates a new and evil-free world. When God determines that it is time, at a time when his people are suffering great persecution from those who are trying to destroy them, he will send Jesus to rescue his people, execute his judgments and justice on the unbelieving peoples of the earth, establish God's holy kingdom, and reign as king over the nations (Acts 3:17-26; Revelation 19:11-16). He will create a new heaven and earth for his people (Isaiah 65:17-25; 2 Peter 3:9-13). His will be an evil-free, love-filled, and righteous kingdom that will never end (Luke 1:30-33). It will exceed all human expectations and bring to people of faith from every nation a satisfying and exciting life beyond all imagination.

As a part of God's story, each of us finds that life is filled with varying degrees of pain and suffering. Though our modern world chooses not to acknowledge it, pain is caused by living in a world full of evil. In each of our stories, living through painful and dark times can make us feel unsure and fearful of what will happen to us. For people who truly trust and follow Christ Jesus, there is always light and hope that nothing can separate us from his love and our ultimate well-being (John 8:12; Romans 8:37-39). God is faithful to fulfill his promised hope (Lamentations 3:19-26; Revelation 21:1-7).

SPECIFIC REASONS GOD WROTE A BOOK

To say, "God wrote a book" is to say that God chose to communicate, in a written document, his story and message to the human race and especially to his people. Much of the Bible is a record of people's experiences with God, allowing us to see what their relationship with God was like and what they learned. God worked through humans who knowingly or unknowingly wrote under the guidance of his Spirit (2 Timothy 3:16; Exodus 17:14; 34:27; 2 Peter 1:21; John 14:26; Revelation 1:1, 9-11). As we examine what they wrote, we shall discover God's specific reasons for writing it. Those reasons are pathways God uses to complete his plans to restore all things. Participating in those reasons helps us identify our part in the story and teaches us how to cooperate with God to bring about his new humanity and world. By reading the following texts and answering the questions, I give the readers an option of discovering God's reasons for themselves before reading my comments.

READ 2 TIMOTHY 3:14-17

Questions:

1. Timothy learned the scriptures from childhood. Did you learn the Bible in your childhood? What did it mean to you?

2. What did the sacred writings give to Timothy? What do the words, *leads to salvation through faith in Christ,* mean to you?

3. What is said in the text about the scriptures?

4. According to the text, what is the purpose of the scriptures?

In 2 Timothy 3:14-17, we discover two key reasons why God wrote a book. First, the sacred writings are able to give wisdom that leads to salvation. Timothy is an example of this. In verse 15 Paul tells us that from childhood, Timothy, one of Paul's trusted and valued coworkers, knew the sacred writings. These writings refer to the Bible's Old Testament because the New Testament had not yet been formed. The Old Testament provided prophecies about a coming Messiah who would be the savior of his people—not only Jews but other people as well. Jesus used these ancient scriptures to explain to his disciples what they said about him (Luke 24:44-47). The disciples used what Jesus taught from the Old Testament to help convince Jewish people that Jesus was the Christ, the central person in God's plan to redeem the world. These sacred writings were what enabled Timothy's mother to know God and have faith in a coming Messiah. Because of the scriptural teachings of his mother (2 Timothy 1:5), Timothy believed in the coming of a Messiah. When he heard, through the Apostle Paul, the good news that the Messiah was a person named Jesus, he believed and experienced God's salvation in Christ.

The second reason for God's Book is to teach, reprove, correct, and train us to do the good deeds God has created us to do (2 Timothy 3:16-17). We are saved to do God's good works as the way to participate with him in overcoming evil and in his healing and restoring of people and their environment (Romans 12:21; Ephesians 2:10). If we could see the full scope of what God's people are doing all over the earth, we would be amazed. Add all of these things together, and we see how God is saving the lives of many people and working to conform them to the ideals of the new world he has planned for them.

For these two reasons, God wrote a book: first, to inform us about his way to be saved from a corrupted and broken life, and second, to equip us to be coworkers in bringing his new world into being.

READ DEUTERONOMY 17:14-20

Questions:

1. When Israel gets a king, he is to make a copy of God's law. What is he to do with it?

2. Why is he to make a copy? What is your practice in using the scriptures?

God wrote a book so the leader of God's people could read it, receive guidance on how to conduct himself, and rightly lead the people. God has given all of us positions of leadership, and his Word helps guide us in leading persons who are under our care. We may not be king of a nation, but we have important responsibilities toward our family, our coworkers, the church, and the world at large, including the care of the earth and the poor and the needy. As followers of Christ Jesus and fellow citizens of his kingdom, we are to cooperate with him in the process of restoring all things, working together to bring God's kingdom to humanity and the earth. In Deuteronomy 17:19-20, we discover five reasons why God wanted the king to read his Word. The reasons apply to us as well.

Reason one: So the king will fear the Lord his God. We too are called to fear the Lord our God. Fearing God is not so much being afraid that he will reprimand or punish us for misdeeds but is more the idea that we have such a high respect and reverence for God that we aspire to know him.

Reason two: So the king will carefully practice all the words of God's law. God's will is revealed in the scriptures so that we can be careful to observe what is good, not only for us, but also to help others (Matthew 7:24-27; 28:19-20). God has given us a handbook describing his job description for successfully living life and serving him. For those who have experienced being made new by his compassion, mercy, and forgiveness, doing his will is a matter of voluntarily serving him because he first loved us (1 John 4:19). We can compare this feeling of loving gratitude toward God to that of a person pulled from a fire, or from drowning. He or she is ever grateful and willing to honor the one who saved him or her (1 Corinthians 6:19-20).

Reason three: So the king's heart may not be lifted up above his fellow citizens. As leaders of others, we are not to lord it over them as if we are better or more important than they are (Luke 18:9-14). We are not to be tyrants, exercising our power over others (Matthew 20:20-28; 1 Peter 5:1-4). We all have different roles to play in life, and although we may be in charge of others' welfare, in God's sight we are coequal in worth, no matter our gender, race, or station in life (Galatians 3:27-29).

Reason four: So the king will not turn away from God's commands. Because we are prone to drift into wrong behaviors and thinking, we need constant reminders (1 Corinthians 10:6-12; Hebrews 2:1; 3:12-13; 2 Peter 3:17-18). It keeps us going in the right direction to keep God's goals before us.

Reason five: So the king and his son may continue their future leadership in Israel. Being sincere followers of God and Christ has promised benefits. Faithfulness to God's calling ensures God's future blessings to us and our offspring (Deuteronomy 6:1-2; Psalm 34:8-14; Ephesians 6:1-3).

READ LUKE 11:28

Questions:

1. What did Jesus say about the Word of God? How has God's Word blessed you?

2. According to the following passages, who are we to listen to and why? (Deuteronomy 18:15-19; Acts 3:22-23; Luke 10:16, 38-42; Matthew 7:24-27; Matthew 28:19-20)

According to Deuteronomy 18 and Acts 3, Jesus is the prophet who is to come, and we are to listen to him. Jesus said our faith and well-being depend on hearing and doing what he says. Jesus believed that we are to live by every word from the mouth of God (Matthew 4:4). He said that the words he speaks to us are life-giving words (John 6:63, 68; 12:47-50).

READ 2 PETER 1:12-21

Questions:

1. Why does Peter say we can believe the things he writes? What does Peter say is true about the prophetic scriptures?

2. What do we learn about why Peter writes this letter?

Peter says, "I will always be ready to remind you of these things, even though you know and have been established in the truth" (2 Peter 1:12-15). As humans, we have a constant need to be reminded of God's way of life, because we forget, and we are carried away with our own needs, wants, and interests. Like the Apostle Paul, I have found that the power of my self-centered life easily corrupts me (Romans 7:14-21). If we are to change into the kind of persons God is creating us to be, we must learn to live by the power of God's Spirit within us. The lures of the world around us are continually feeding us things to satisfy our fleshly nature. We need the words of God to continually feed our spiritual nature so we walk in the Spirit and live like Christ (Galatians 5:16-17). Reading the Bible daily keeps me close to God and reminds me of who I am in Christ and how God wants me to live my life.

READ PSALM 119:9-11, 28, 38, 49-52, 98-100, 105, 133, 162, 165; JOSHUA 1:8

Questions:

1. According to these scriptures, why is the Bible important?

2. Can you tell stories of times these verses operated/ happened in your life?

The above verses describe many benefits that come from reading and believing God's Word. For example, God's Book will help us keep our life pure, develop reverence for God, enlighten us with understanding and guidance for successful living, be revived in the face of adversity, and so forth. Here are a couple of stories of how these verses worked in my own life. Perhaps they will help you recall a story or two of your own.

Concerning God's Word producing reverence for God (Psalm 119:38), I share this experience. I lied to someone, and when I got home, my conscience bothered me because God's Word says not to lie (Colossians 3:9). I knew God wanted me to go back and tell the person what I did. My pride fought it, and I wrestled with God for what seemed like hours. Finally, I thought, *OK, I will do it.* The next day I went to the person and told him how I had lied to him. He asked me why I had come to tell him. I answered that I have a relationship with God, and I did not want to damage it. He was surprised at my answer but accepted my apology. I learned that to reverence God meant to respect his Word and to honor him by obeying what he wanted me to do.

One other story is how God comforted me with his Word (Psalm 19:49-52). I had a close friend. We got together every week and knew one another quite well. We had many conversations about the Christian faith and what it meant to become a believer in Christ

Jesus. After a couple of years, he told me he had decided to trust his life to Jesus. One day, he died in an accident. Rumor around town was that he committed suicide. He had problems, but I knew him enough to doubt he would do such a thing. However, the thought disturbed me and I could not sleep. I needed to be comforted and have my mind be at peace (Psalm 119:49-52). I picked up my Bible and read a statement by the Apostle Paul. He said that if he did wrong, "I am no longer the one doing it, but sin which dwells in me" (Romans 7:20). I thought, *When I sin I say I did it, but Paul says it was not him.* Suddenly, I realized it was because he was no longer the person he used to be; he was a new creation in Christ. Even if my friend had taken his own life, he had a new nature, and it was not him doing it. I thanked God, for the truth of his Word gave me peace. Know this, however: such truth does not excuse anyone's actions (Romans 6:1-2); it only says God's forgiveness is stronger than our sin (Romans 8:1).

READ 1 CORINTHIANS 10:1-12

Questions:

1. The Bible relates a history of earth's people. What is the purpose of knowing things about them?

2. What do each of the five examples listed in verses 6-10 mean for you?

God includes in his Word a history of people's experiences, good and bad, which serve as examples. Things we learn from history will benefit us if we heed them. One thing we learn is that whatever happens to people always has something to do with the kind of relationship they have, or don't have, with God (Psalm 119:155). People who are bad examples help us see what not to do. We want to avoid making similar mistakes and avoid the sufferings they bring. Good examples can encourage us to see how valuable it is to live right (1 Corinthians 4:14-17). God's Book tells us about real people and real life. Reading these examples shows how our everyday lives are influenced by each other, whether for good or bad (1 Corinthians 15:33). Reading stories of good people's lives is like hanging out with them and receiving encouragement to live according to God's righteous ways.

READ LUKE 1:1-4 (ACTS 1:1); 2 CORINTHIANS 2:4; 1 PETER 5:12; 1 JOHN 1:1-4, 5:13; PROVERBS 1:1-5

Question:

- Pause after reading each passage and discuss why you think the reason presented by the writer is important.

Much of the time, the Bible contains statements like, "The word of the Lord came to . . ." or, "The Lord said . . ." or, "Hear the word of the Lord." These kinds of statements indicate that the writers are receiving their messages directly from the Lord. At other times, like in the references above, the writers give personal reasons for writing, perhaps without knowing they are under the inspiration of the Holy Spirit (John 14:26; 16:12-15). These reasons by individual writers are to be regarded as worthy of our notice. For example, Luke investigated and wrote in order to pass on accurate information about the eyewitness accounts of Jesus and the early church. Paul says he wrote out of much concern for fellow believers so they would know of the love he has for them. Peter wrote to exhort and testify to the true grace of God. John wrote a letter to share what he and the other apostles saw and heard concerning Jesus so the believers could have fellowship together and with God the Father and the Son. He also wrote so believers would know with certainty that they possess eternal life. The writer of Proverbs wrote to give naïve and inexperienced people instruction in wise behavior. Their personal reasons for writing, if heeded, produce significant experiences for us.

READ JOHN 20:30-31

Questions:

1. What two reasons does John give for writing?
2. We see road signs and other signs every day. What is the purpose of a sign?

"These things" (signs from Jesus), said John, "have been written so that you may believe that Jesus is the Christ, the Son of God; and that believing you may have life in his name." Apart from the Bible, how much do we know about Jesus, the Messiah (Christ)? As popular as he was during his short-lived time on earth, there is hardly a word mentioned about him in any secular historical documents. Without God's Book, we would know little or nothing about Christ Jesus. Yet he is, without doubt, the most unique and highly-to-be-regarded person who ever lived. His importance to the entire world is summed up in one sentence written by one of his disciples. John wrote, "The Father has sent the Son to be the savior of the world" (1 John 4:14). The truth is, without Jesus, the world has nothing to offer.

Incorporated into God's writings are clues (signs) that tell us to be on the lookout for a person who will come and set all things right. The Old Testament writers give testimony to a promised Messiah (Genesis 3:15; Isaiah 53:4-5; Micah 5:2; Zechariah 14:1-9). New Testament companions and eyewitness observers of Jesus give testimony to him as that Messiah (Christ), the one who has now come to complete God's real-life story (Luke 9:18-22; Revelation 19:11-16). Jesus is the one and only person to guarantee a happy ending for all who place their hope in him (Revelation 1:4-7; 22:12-14, 20). Why did God write a book? He wrote to tell us the gospel of Jesus, which is the good news found throughout the Bible of the one who saved the world and all who believe.

READ JEREMIAH 30:1-3 (36:1-3); ISAIAH 53:3-6 (ACTS 3:13-18); ZECHARIAH 14:1-5; MATTHEW 24:21-31 (ROMANS 15:4, 12-13); ISAIAH 13:6-13 (REVELATION 6:12-17); 2 PETER 3:10-14 (PSALM 102:25-26); REVELATION 1:1-3, 17-19 (21:1-7)

Questions:

1. What is your picture of God's plans?

2. How does knowing the future affect a person's life?

All the above references have a message in common: that God wrote a book to tell us things to expect in the future. The Bible tells us about coming events for a number of reasons. One reason is so we can know God has spoken the truth. When God says something is going to happen, and it happens, we know that the words spoken and written by the prophets of God are truly from God (Deuteronomy 18:15-22). When we trust the certainty of God's Word, we cannot be shaken (Psalm 16:8-9; 55:22). There are prophets whose signs or wonders may come true, but if they lead us to pursue a god other than the God of the Bible, we are not to listen to that prophet (Deuteronomy 13:1-5).

A second reason God tells us about coming events is so we can have hope when we think all is falling apart in our lives and world. Giving hope to people is a huge purpose for God's writings. God has a plan for the world that will certainly happen, for he has the power to make it happen. Our hope is in Christ, who will restore all things and give us rest from all troubles, turmoil, and pain caused by evils (Isaiah 14:3, 7; 32:17-18; Matthew 11:28-30; Acts 3:17-21). We have a guaranteed future, and faith in these things will give us joy and peace in the midst of adversity and troublesome times.

A third reason for revealing the future is so we will not be surprised by what God says is coming, but we will be prepared and ready for it (Matthew 24:42-44; 25:1-13; 1 Thessalonians 5:1-11; 2 Peter 3:11-14).

A WRITTEN WORD MAKES SENSE

Could God have gotten his points across to humanity without a carefully preserved written record? Of course, but most of us moderns would find it difficult to trust a message conveyed throughout the centuries by word of mouth alone. Most would question its historical accuracy. A case in point, made by highly respected historian Kenneth C. Davis, is that "much of what we remember about our history is either mistaken or fabricated." Davis continues, "Our historical sense is frequently skewed, skewered, or plain screwed up by myths and misconceptions."[3]

I suppose God could make his truth known to every individual by supernatural means, as he has done for some, including the prophets and writers of holy scripture. But many in this world claim to have received a word from God, and when the accounts are contradictory, who are we to believe? Obviously, for good reason,

---

3. Kenneth C. Davis, *Don't Know Much About History* (New York: Harper Collins, 2003), xv-xvi & xvii.

God prefers a testable and reliable written record to communicate and preserve his messages. A claim the Bible sets forth is that God was involved in his writings through the activity of his Holy Spirit (2 Timothy 3:16; 2 Peter 1:16-21; Acts 2:23-31). If that is true, as evidenced in many ways, we have no reason to doubt his message.

We Christians believe that the original manuscripts of the Bible were without error, but currently, all we have are *copies* of the originals. Some would use that to convince us that the Bible has errors. I am not claiming there are no mistakes in the copies we have of the Bible, only that they have been identified and found to be few (less than 1 percent of the entire text) and minor, and in no way do they corrupt or hinder the truths God has made known to us. When it comes to trusting the accuracy of the Bible, there are many skeptics. I am glad I was one of them, for it caused me to search out answers to verify for myself whether or not God's Word can be trusted. I have complete confidence in the accuracy and trustworthiness of God's Word. Skepticism can be a good thing when it protects us from things that can harm us, but skepticism can also keep us from believing things that are good for us.

THE RELATIONSHIP BETWEEN THE BIBLE AND FAITH

The Bible contains energy in its words, energy that awakens faith in a person's life—energy that produces its intended results. Hebrews 4:12 says, "The word of God is living and active." God said in the Old Testament that his Word would not return to him empty. When a word proceeds from God's mouth, it accomplishes what he desires it to do (Isaiah 55:11). The Apostle Paul said he was not ashamed of speaking the gospel of Christ Jesus to people. He says these words are the power of God for salvation to all who believe (Romans 1:16). Paul said, "Faith comes from hearing, and hearing by the word of Christ" (Romans 10:17). In Creation, when God spoke, things came into being. So it is when we hear and believe the Word of God about Jesus, we become a new creation in Christ (2 Corinthians 5:17).

Herein is a key to experiencing the power of God's Word: we must respond to God's Word with faith. Peter connects faith with the

Word of God when he says that by believing in Christ, we obtain the outcome of our faith, the salvation of our souls (1 Peter 1:8-9, 23, 25). The writer of the book of Hebrews makes this same point. "We have had the good news preached to us, just as they also [Old Testament Israelites]; but the word they heard did not profit them, because it was not united by faith in those who heard" (Hebrews 4:2). The Apostle Paul said that when we believe the Word of God, it performs its work in us (1 Thessalonians 2:13).

Jesus told a story about God's Word and four kinds of people (Matthew 13:3-9, 18-23; Luke 8:4-15). A farmer sowed seed and it landed on four types of soil, representing four types of people. The seed was the Word of God. Some heard the words, but did not believe them, so they did not experience God's salvation. Some believed the words and accepted them with great joy, but they never deepened their faith, and so when temptations came, they fell away. Some who heard allowed their worldly pursuits to govern their lives and did not live out their faith as God intended, so no God-honoring lifestyle was produced. Others heard the Word with an honest and good heart, held onto it with strong faith, and with perseverance bore much fruit. In this parable, the effectiveness of God's Word depends on the measure of a person's faith. For those who are honest about their need for God and who desperately want his help, the Word of God ignites a sincere faith that brings its good and everlasting results into their lives.

The Bible is not the object of our faith; rather, God, and what he does for us, is the object of our faith. His Book is only a catalyst to move us into a relationship with God so that by his Spirit, he can transform our lives through faith, hope, and love (Romans 5:1-5). God guides us by his Word so that we can grow to be a blessing to the world around us. Remember, when God's reasons for writing a book become our purpose for reading and living, we improve our own lives and the lives of those around us, and we are involved in working with God toward his goal of restoring his coming new world.

CHAPTER 3

HOW STRONG IS YOUR FAITH?

I n the first chapter, we defined faith as having three aspects: an object, an agreement with the object, a commitment (surrendering) of one's life to the object. We used two biblical words, *the faith*, to include the good news (gospel) of Christ Jesus, the Bible as God's true story, and nature's revelation of God. These three supply the all-encompassing content of Christian faith which, by faith, we commit our lives to. We also noted that without faith, we limit life, for we will not know or experience the good and necessary things that life offers. In this chapter, by examining the faith of people mentioned in the Bible, we will be challenged to think about the strength of *our own* faith. If you are Christian, how strong is your faith?

LITTLE FAITH

The phrase, "You of little faith" is used by Jesus during his message on the subject of worry (Matthew 6:25-34; Luke 12:22-32). He warned against stressing over a lack of food, clothing, and other necessities of life. He tells us we cannot change anything by worrying and fretting. He tells us how valuable we are to God. He tells us God knows what we need and he will certainly take care of us. He also says life consists of more than material needs; that above all else, we are to seek God's kingdom and his righteousness. When we do not know God the Father and Son as our all-powerful benevolent ruler and greatest treasure, and when we miss the truth of our great worth to God and of his loving care for us, then, when we encounter life's hardships, we open ourselves to being fearful, worried, and anxious. We have *little faith*. However, if what we treasure is found in the realm of God, not in earthly things, and if our true master is from the heavenly realm, not the earthly (Proverbs 23:4-5; Matthew 6:19-21, 24), then our faith will grow beyond being little.

Fearful, life-threatening events often test the strength of our faith. Jesus and his disciples were in a boat during a raging storm at sea. Fearing for their lives, they woke Jesus from sleep, crying out, "Save us, Lord; we are perishing." Jesus responded, "Why are you afraid, you men of *little faith*?" (emphasis added). Then he spoke and calmed the wind and sea (Matthew 8:23-27; Luke 8:22-27). The response of his disciples was, "Who is this?" Why were the disciples fearful, and why was Jesus able to be at peace? Obviously, the disciples did not know Jesus, and they did not see what Jesus saw. What he saw was how big God is, how great a love he has for us, and his promised plans for us as his children. *Little faith* does not know Jesus and does not see what he sees.

On another occasion, in a boat on a windy night at sea, Jesus came walking on the water to join the disciples. Thinking it was a ghost, they were overwhelmed by sudden fear. Jesus identified himself and told them not to be afraid. Peter decided to find out if it was Jesus and told Jesus to command him to walk to him on the water. Jesus told him to come. Peter was doing OK until he felt the force of the wind and began to sink. Jesus grabbed his hand, pulled him up, and said, "You of *little faith*, why did you doubt?" (emphasis added). *Little faith* focuses on our problems instead of on the presence and hope Jesus offers. What difference does it make to have the Lord present with us? One difference for the disciples was that when Jesus got into the boat, the wind stopped (Matthew 14:22-33). When the presence of the Lord is realized so that we are not shaken by fearful happenings and the threatening storms of life, we will have gotten beyond *little faith* (Acts 2:25; Psalm 16:8-9).

One day, while on a journey with Jesus, the disciples heard him say something about leaven, and they became concerned over the fact that they had forgotten to bring bread. Again Jesus said, "You men of *little faith*, why do you discuss among yourselves that you have no bread?" (emphasis added). He reminded them of the times he fed thousands of people by miraculously multiplying small quantities of food (Matthew 16:5-12). In light of what God empowered him to do, there was no need to worry about physical bread. Furthermore, they had misunderstood Jesus's comment about leaven. He was not talking about bread but about the need to avoid the false and dangerous teachings of their religious leaders. *Little faith* meant they still had not seen who Jesus was, and because of this, they were focused too much on the physical aspects of life and not enough on the spiritual things Jesus was trying to teach them.

It was important for Jesus's disciples to learn who he was and to get beyond *little faith* because their future job would be to proclaim and explain him to the world. They must be convinced in their own minds that he is the Son of God, the long-promised Christ (Messiah), who God the Father sent to rescue people from their sin and from this corrupt evil world (Matthew 16:13-16). Jesus needed his disciples to overcome their *little faith* because, in addition to telling the world who he was, they must also learn to believe God for his power to perform miracles. Doing miracles similar to what Jesus did would verify that what they proclaimed about Jesus was true, thus persuading and drawing others to believe in him (Matthew 10:1-8; Mark 6:12-13; Acts 2:43; Hebrews 2:3-4).

What does having faith in Jesus mean for us who are living in today's world? Are we to think that by faith we can have Jesus miraculously provide food when we are hungry, or rescue us from dangers whenever our lives are threatened? It is true that miraculous signs and wonders through God's people also occur today at various times and in various places. My wife experienced a miraculous healing from God; so have I, and so have many other people. In no way do I belittle the right to seek God for healing and daily provisions here and now, but let us not be discouraged if miracles do not happen for us, for God has a greater purpose for our faith than to take away all our trials and pains in this life.

More than looking to God for a miracle to get us out of suffering (which is not wrong), we are to focus on the miracle of God's salvation. Jesus sent seventy people to go out to tell others about the kingdom of God, heal people of their diseases, and cast out demons. They came back, rejoicing that the power of God, through them, healed many people. Jesus then reminded them, "Do not rejoice in this, that evil spirits are subject to you, but rejoice that your names are recorded in heaven" (Luke 10:1, 9, 17-20). The main goal or outcome of our faith is our salvation. The greatest miracle God does is to cause people to be born again to a living hope, to an inheritance imperishable and undefiled that will not fade away (1 Peter 1:3-9). *Little faith* focuses on lesser things, the temporary things of this earthly life. *Greater faith* sets the mind on things above, not on the things that are on the earth (Colossians 3:1-4; Matthew 16:21-23).

God's salvation, however, does not just enable us to look forward to the hope of heaven. Salvation is past, present, and future. Salvation *past* is when we died and came to life in Christ Jesus, a time when we received his Spirit of love, forgiveness, and eternal life (Ephesians 2:1-5). Salvation *present* is God transforming our lives from one degree of glory to another, making us more like Jesus (2 Corinthians 3:18; Galatians 4:19). His transforming of our lives means growing in love and holiness, doing his will, enjoying the things he gives us, and experiencing victories over sin (Philippians 2:12-13; 1 John 3:2-3). Salvation *future* is our glorious entrance into the eternal kingdom of our Lord and Savior Jesus Christ (2 Peter 1:1-11). God is faithful to complete his work of salvation in us (Philippians 1:6). His perfecting of our lives may require us to endure trials and sufferings along the way, but when we accept our sufferings and have faith and joy in God's work to complete us (Philippians 3:10-11; James 1:2-4), we are overcoming *little faith*.

WEAK FAITH

The Apostle Paul says in Romans 14:1, "Now accept the one who is *weak in faith*." What does he mean? Early in my walk with God I came across Christians who believed differently than I did. What they told me challenged my faith. *Are they right? Am I wrong? Is that what the Bible really says?* Evidently, according to their understanding of God's Word, when I became a believer in Jesus, I may have been saved, but I did not have the fullness of the Holy Spirit. The proof that I did not have the Holy Spirit was that I had not spoken in tongues (Acts 2:4; 10:44-48; 19:6). I remember the struggle I had trying to understand the "baptism of the Holy Spirit." I thought I had it right, but this teaching bothered my conscience, and I felt my faith was lacking and that I was not the Christian I needed to be. I seriously prayed and earnestly pleaded with God to give me his Holy Spirit, proven by speaking in tongues. God was not answering, so I was told to step out in faith, just start speaking, and tongues would come. I tried it, trusting God to give me his Spirit, but over time, nothing happened, and I felt my faith was deficient.

Why was God not blessing me with his promised Spirit and power? He knew I wholeheartedly wanted it. This whole process produced uncertainty about God's truth and shook my faith. What was I lacking that God was not giving me his Holy Spirit? After all, Jesus said in Luke 11:13, "If you know how to give good gifts to your children, how much more will your heavenly Father give the Holy Spirit to those who ask him?" Apparently, I had *weak faith*. My ability to believe God must be lacking.

Originally, I felt I had a strong faith because I believed the gospel and I believed I had the Holy Spirit, but now I doubted my faith, and I felt judged by others as an incomplete Christian. It was causing me to question my relationship and good standing with other believers and with God. I spent a year reading books and studying the Bible, asking God to show me the truth about "the baptism of the Holy Spirit." In the end, I believed the Bible taught that I received the Holy Spirit when I trusted Jesus to save me, and I did not need tongues as a proof;[4] rather, I needed to have faith that the Holy Spirit was in me because I had Jesus in me (John 14:16-18; Ephesians 1:13; Galatians 3:2). When I came to believe this was the teaching of God's Word, I now differed from other believers in my belief. Since we believed differently, my question was, *How should believers who do not agree respond to each other?*

---

4. There is a difference between the baptism of the Holy Spirit and the gifts of the Spirit. I believe God can give the gift of speaking in tongues to believers, but speaking in tongues as an evidence of the baptism of the Spirit is a different matter.

Isn't that what Paul is trying to teach us when he says to accept the one who is *weak in faith* (Romans 14:1)?

As we explore God's teachings in Romans 14, we discover there are objective and subjective aspects involved in *weak faith*. The objective aspect dealt with in this passage is the ethical and theological issue about what God says we can eat. The issue states, "One person has faith that he may eat all things, but he who is *weak [in faith]* eats vegetables only" (Romans 14:2). This verse is not dealing with choosing to eat the right foods for better health. First Corinthians 8:4-7 gives us a more specific background. Some Christians believed that to eat meat offered as a sacrifice to idols was not wrong because there is only one true God, and idols (other gods) do not really exist; therefore, it is OK to eat meat offered to idols.[5] However, not all have this knowledge. *Weak faith* means that the person eating vegetables and rejecting meat misunderstands and lacks God's revealed truth on this issue. A person with *weak faith* needs accurate information about *the faith*, thus forming the objective content of their belief. Actually, all Christians most likely fit this scenario in that we all need additional information to bring what we believe more in line with the truths of God's Word.

Subjectively, *weak faith* involves a person's conscience (1 Corinthians 8:7-12). These unenlightened Corinthians actually and sincerely believed in their hearts that it was wrong to eat meat sacrificed to idols. Therefore, when other believers told them it is OK to eat the meat, it bothered their conscience. Putting doubts in their minds and hearts and leaving them with confusion and guilt caused them to have *weak faith*, meaning they felt unsure of the way God wanted them to live. Added to that, they felt rejected by the rest of the believing community unless they changed their views. This uncertainty and non-acceptance created a block in their confident walk with Christ. If not resolved, would it put them in danger of slipping back into sin or leaving fellow believers with whom they disagreed and going their own way?

---

5. For more detailed information explaining the cultural issues involving Greeks and Jews eating food offered to idols, here are two resources that you can consult: Kenneth E. Bailey, *Paul Through Mediterranean Eyes: Cultural Studies in 1 Corinthians* (Downers Grove, IL: InterVarsity Press, Academic, 2011), 229-241; Peter H. Davids, *More Hard Sayings of the New Testament* (Downers Grove, IL: InterVarsity Press, 1991), 62-66.

When told I did not have the Holy Spirit because I had not spoken in tongues, my conscience bothered me. My *faith became weak* because I lost the certainty of what I believed and began doing all I could to speak in tongues. When that failed, I began a diligent search in the Bible to see what it said. I felt like an unaccepted citizen in the church, and not until I was convinced in my mind and heart of what the Bible taught did I have my faith restored and strengthened (Romans 14:22-23).

Resolving the issue for myself, however, still left me with the issue of how to develop loving oneness with those who disagreed with my belief and practice. What do we do when issues of what to believe and how to practice our faith differ from others? Paul, in Romans 14, gives the principles of how God wants us to resolve issues like this. These principles apply to the people on both sides and tell them how they need to handle their relationships so that loving oneness can be maintained in the body of Christ (John 17:20-21; Ephesians 4:1-3). Looking more closely at Romans 14 will help us understand what Paul is teaching.

Paul says there needs to be acceptance of the one we disagree with (Romans 14:1). Paul says the one who is strong in faith is not to have contempt for the one with *weak faith,* and the one with *weak faith* is not to judge as wrong the one who has strong faith (Romans 14:3). As he continues, we see the reason why he tells them not to judge each other and treat each other with contempt. The reason is that God has accepted each of them, and who are we to judge a servant of God (Romans 14:3-4, 10-12)? As long as each is convinced they are serving God and glorifying him with their lives and not living for themselves, and as long as they both believe Christ died for them and they are faithfully trying to serve him, then they are to love and accept one another (Romans 15:5-7).

Rather than judge one another, we should be concerned not to put an obstacle or stumbling block in a fellow believer's way (Romans 14:13, 21). Don't hurt or destroy each other with your judgments and contempt; rather, walk according to love, for the kingdom of God is one of righteousness, peace, and joy in the Holy Spirit (Romans 14:15-18). Since we all belong to Christ, let's build one another up and not tear down the work of God because of these kinds of disagreements (Romans 14:19-21). In other words, all are convinced they are following what Jesus would have them do, and God will be the final judge. Each is allowed to have his or her own conviction before God so long as each is not doubting and condemning him or herself (Romans 14:22-23).

I used the wording of Romans 14:3 to help me deal with differences I had with those who believed in speaking in tongues as necessary for the baptism of the Holy Spirit. I substituted the issue we differed about in place of the food issue. For example, I read the verse this way: "The one who speaks in tongues is not to regard with contempt the one who does not speak in tongues, and the one who does not speak in tongues is not to judge the one who does speak in tongues, for God has accepted him or her." Many issues of disagreement where one Christian believes a certain practice is OK for him or her, and the other does not, can substitute their issue into this verse as a way to preserve love and oneness. Examples of other issues might include social drinking of beer or wine, going to movies, worshiping on Saturday or Sunday, letting your kids observe Halloween, differing views like Premillennialism versus Amillennialism or Calvinism versus Arminianism, issues concerning water baptism, and so forth. The goal is to keep from causing others to stumble in their faith (Romans 14:13, 20-21) by being willing to forgo the right to force your beliefs in situations you know would hurt or offend them. Perhaps *weak faith* applies to persons on both sides, if either side fails to practice the principles taught in Romans 14.

Does this mean there is no room for helping one another re-examine our viewpoints? Not at all. We should welcome others to share their opinions or views and listen to their reasons for believing and practicing them. I've said to people in the church that it's OK to differ from each other and to hold strong to your views of scripture, but be open to hearing and learning from each other. We can grow and possibly gain a more accurate view of God's truth through the challenges others present to us about our faith. It's OK to doubt or struggle with our beliefs until we come to a position on what scripture says. It's also OK not to believe one way or the other on certain issues that are not clear in scripture or are not necessary for salvation.

By sharing with others, a person may see reasons for changing his or her views, similar to the case involving Apollos, Priscilla, and Aquila (Acts 18:24-26). Understanding and practicing Romans 14 will go a long way to practicing a love that prevents hard feelings, does not treat fellow believers with contempt and rejection, and avoids unnecessary splits in churches. I am reminded of what Jesus said when his disciples pointed to others who were doing God's work but were not following along with them. Jesus said, "Do not hinder them ... for he who is not against us is for us" (Mark 9:38-40).[6]

Because believers in Jesus lack love and unity over differing beliefs, unbelievers often have difficulty accepting the Christian message. If Jesus teaches love and unity among believers, how can there be so many divisions in the church? It is a good point, and although differences sometimes prove to be useful in enhancing God's work, they are often out of sync with the Lord's prayer that we be one (John 17:20-23). Jesus did command us to love one another so that people would know we are his disciples (John 13:34-35). It is certainly expected, and not necessarily bad, that Christians will differ from one another in their understanding of the faith, but this ought not prevent friendly relationships in the love and unity of God's Spirit (Ephesians 4:1-6). By God's grace, we need to learn how to accept one another, even with differences, for God seemingly allows them.

DEAD FAITH

Dead faith is described in these words: "Faith without works is dead" (James 2:26). James says that we demonstrate our faith by the works we do (James 2:18). Faith in Jesus Christ and the loving relationship we have with him will work itself out by doing the good works of God (John 14:12). What good is it to have faith in God if it does not produce anything valuable and beneficial? The Apostle Paul reminds us that we are saved by faith and not by works but quickly adds that we are created in Christ Jesus for good works (Ephesians 2:8-10). The Bible commends believers for their "work of faith" (1 Thessalonians 1:3). How do we know that

---

6. Note: A different situation and form of weak faith is identified and discussed below under the heading of "Great Faith; Strong Faith," where weak faith and strong faith are mentioned in Romans 4:19-20.

we have true faith in God and Christ Jesus? If faith is real, it will show itself with visible actions. Doing the works of God proves the genuineness of our faith.

What enables us to do good works? When we put our faith in Jesus, we are born into (John 3:3-7), adopted into (Galatians 4:4-7), and transferred into his kingdom (Colossians 1:13-14). We became partakers of God's divine nature, having escaped the corruption that is in the world (2 Peter 1:4). We've experienced God's love (1 John 4:19), and Jesus is our example of what love looks like. Since this is what Christians have experienced and know to be true, then out of a new heart of love, we find ourselves growing away from self-centeredness, voluntarily choosing to do God's good works, and furthering his kingdom on earth. Having received God's life, we now ask God to demonstrate his kind of life through us in a way that will benefit the lives of others. This may sometimes happen in the form of miracles, even such as Jesus did during his earthly visit, but mostly it happens by doing what is good and loving others as Jesus did.

Dead faith describes a person who says he or she believes in God and Jesus but does little or nothing to show God's love toward others. Jesus came into the world to show us what God is like (Hebrews 1:3), to tell us about God's kingdom (Matthew 4:23), and to demonstrate what life looks like when God's kingdom is present. The works Jesus did among us showed that the kingdom of God had come to earth, though not yet in its completed form. Our good works show the same thing. We each have a part in God's overall plan to rid the world of evil and restore all things to goodness (Romans 12:14-21).

UNSURE FAITH

A man wanted Jesus to heal his son and said, "If you can do anything, take pity on us and help us" (Mark 9:20-24). Jesus responded to the man with a question and a statement: "'If you can?' All things are possible to him who believes." Immediately, the boy's father replied, "I do believe; *help my unbelief.*" *Unsure faith* is faith where belief and unbelief are both present. Many of us have a mixture of belief and skepticism in our faith. This man's problem seemed to be that he was not sure who Jesus was, thus Jesus's question, "If you can?" When we know that Jesus is the Son of God and the Creator of the world and everything in it, then we have no question that Jesus has power and goodness to do great things. This man's unbelief questioned Jesus and Jesus's capabilities, and at the same time, he pleaded for Jesus to strengthen his faith—to take away his doubts. When Jesus healed his son, this helped the man have a stronger faith. We could put Thomas's doubting of Jesus in a similar category (John 20:24-29). Unless he saw for himself, he was hesitant to believe others' witness that Jesus was alive. How gracious of God when he gives us convincing reasons to believe in him. God desires that we have a strong and sure faith.

These cases differ from the man who asked Jesus if he would heal him of leprosy. This leper had no doubt about the identity and power of Jesus; rather, his doubt, for whatever reason—perhaps a feeling of unworthiness—was whether or not Jesus was willing to heal him (Luke 5:12-13). I often have the same thought: *I know God can heal, but I am not always sure he will do it in my case.* It may not be his will. It may be his will for the problem to remain, as with the Apostle Paul when he prayed three times for God to help him, but to no avail. To Paul, God said that his grace was sufficient, and God allowed the problem to remain as a way to aid the development of Paul's Christian character (2 Corinthians 12:5-10).

When Jesus prayed for God to take the cross from him, he added, "Yet not what I will, but what You will" (Mark 14:32-36). Jesus knew God could save him from this evil event, but if death on the cross was what God wanted him to do, he was willing to accept God's will, no matter how difficult. It is very possible to believe with absolute certainty that God can do what we ask, but it may not be God's will in our situation, and he does not answer the request as we want. Paul and Jesus knew why God denied their requests, and if we can accept that God has good reason for denying our requests, it helps immensely in the acceptance of his will and in overcoming unsure faith.

FAILING FAITH

Failing faith is a faith which, for various reasons, is plagued with doubts. Such faith could either revive or fall into unbelief and become shipwrecked. When Peter denied Jesus, he felt so bad that it must have been easy for him to think Jesus would disown him as he wondered how Jesus could still love him. I've felt that way when I fail Jesus. Jesus, knowing Peter would deny him, prayed for Peter that his *faith would not fail* (Luke 22:31-34). *Does Jesus pray that for me too?* Prayer keeps us involved with God when dark times come. Peter's faith did not fail, partly because he kept hanging around with fellow believers. It paid off, because he was with them when Jesus appeared later. At that time, Jesus's conversation and love for Peter restored and strengthened his faith. Peter had no reason to give up the faith, for he was convinced there was no one like Jesus worthy of committing his life to.

Others, however, suffer shipwreck regarding their faith (1 Timothy 1:18-19; 6:20-21). They listen to convincing talk from those who present good-sounding arguments against God, and in time, as they entertain these implanted doubts, they experience *failing faith* and go away from *the faith*. It can easily happen over time that any number of things can convince us to doubt and stop believing. For example, we can be convinced by atheistic thinkers that God does not exist or care about us, or by experiencing hardships and sufferings, or by unanswered prayers, or by apparent contradictions in the Bible that cause us to wonder if God's Word is true.

As we wrestle with these and other potentially life-shattering issues, our faith can be shaken and in danger of being shipwrecked. Admittedly, life can present us with some tough questions, but it is always wise to search for answers from the other side before giving up on God and our faith (Proverbs 18:17). Of course, one must know where to look. To lose one's faith in God is not good, especially if God exists, promises to be there for us, and rewards our faith. Rejecting such a powerful source of help during life's critical times would be a foolish thing to do. In light of weaker or less rewarding options, finding what will strengthen our faith is the wise thing to do.[7]

---

7. *Christian Apologetics in the Postmodern World*, edited by Timothy R. Phillips & Dennis L Okholm (Downers Grove, IL: InterVarsity Press, 1995), would be one good resource for beginning ideas on where to find help.

SINCERE FAITH

Sincere faith is mentioned in 2 Timothy 1:5, where Paul writes that he is mindful of Timothy's *sincere faith*. Timothy had help in developing this kind of faith because he grew up having *sincere faith* modeled for him by his mother and grandmother. First Timothy 1:5 says that "the goal of [Christian] instruction is love from a pure heart and a good conscience and a *sincere faith*." This verse tells us that our goal is to love as Jesus loves—and this love comes from three sources: a pure heart, a good conscience, and *a sincere faith*.

What is *sincere faith*? *Sincere faith* means it is real, not put on as a show to make one look good, not being Christian in name only, not faking it by pretending, not being hypocritical; rather, faith is genuine. It is based on a firm conviction that God is real and his Word is true (1 Thessalonians 2:13). *Sincere faith* means a deep, abiding personal surrender to God and a desire to live by the teachings of God. As Jesus told his disciples, they are to teach people to practice his words, not just believe and hold onto them as true doctrines (Matthew 28:20). If a person's faith is real and sincere, the love of God will come forth in daily living, and others will notice godly deeds of unexpected goodness, kindness, and mercy.

A cook at an elementary school was talking about a teacher who voluntarily showed up before school every morning. With a positive attitude, this teacher helped serve the children breakfast, lovingly disciplined the children's behavior, and complimented the cooks for their hard work. She also went beyond expectations by helping to clean up afterwards. Many non-Christians could do the same, but the cook, who knew of the teacher's Christian affiliations, commented about her, "Now there is a real Christian." People who are experiencing God's love and who practice that love are those with sincere faith (James 1:22; 2:15-17; Ezekiel 33:30-31). The Apostle Paul sent Timothy to help new believers and recommended him with these words: "I have no one else of kindred spirit who will *genuinely be concerned for your welfare*. For they all seek after their own interests, not those of Christ Jesus" (Philippians 2:20-21). *Sincere faith* truly acts like God by loving others in practical ways (1 John 4:20-21; Luke 10:30-37).

GREAT FAITH; STRONG FAITH

Great faith is attributed to at least two persons Jesus met. One was a Roman centurion who highly regarded his slave who was about to die. He heard about Jesus and sent some Jewish elders to find him, ask him to come to his home, and heal his beloved servant. While on his way, Jesus received a message from this humble, unworthy-minded centurion, saying that Jesus did not need to come, but just say the word and the healing of his servant would happen. Jesus commented to the crowd that "not even in Israel have I found such *great faith*" (Luke 7:2-10).

What is great faith, and what made this man's faith so much greater than that of others, especially God's people, the Israelites? Jesus said his faith surpassed that of the Israelites, probably because the Israelites had difficulty believing that Jesus was their promised Messiah. For example, in Jesus's hometown, many took offense at him and he could not do many miracles there because of their unbelief (Matthew 13:54-58). Jesus spent about three years trying to convince Jewish people that God sent him to be their savior, doing many miracles as evidence of this truth, and in the end, they crucified him. Even his closest disciples did not understand and believe his word that if killed, he would rise from the dead.

Yet this centurion, who apparently had not personally seen Jesus or heard his teachings, believed that Jesus had authority from a higher source to do miracles. He likely concluded this from hearing reports about him. Not only that, but he believed that his authority to heal did not require his presence at the scene but could be accomplished simply by speaking a word. How many people in our day hear reports of miracles and are skeptical? They think there must be some natural way to explain them. Jesus said, "Blessed are they who did not see, and yet believed" (John 20:29). Jesus marveled at the greatness of this man's unwavering faith. He unreservedly believed that whatever Jesus spoke would happen, even if it seemed contrary to reason or possibility.

The centurion asked Jesus to come to his home to heal his servant, but for some reason he changed his mind, apparently feeling unworthy for Jesus to come. I have often wondered if there are factors that enter into God's honoring a person's faith. I know the Bible says God is no respecter of persons, that he shows no favoritism (Acts 10:34-35; Romans 2:11), but it also says he judges the wicked and gives grace to the humble (James 4:6). This centurion knew he did not deserve God's grace. Is true humility a factor influencing God's decision to help? Consider Jesus's story in Luke 18:9-14. God hears the prayer of the humble person. Pride can hinder God's working in a person's life (2 Kings 5:9-14). The centurion, in addition to humility, also had compassion and love toward his servant and wanted to see him well. Does God look at the heart of one who asks his help? James says that if we ask with wrong motives we do not receive what we ask (James 4:3). There are undoubtedly many factors determining how and why God answers prayer. Does God's answer to the centurion's request indicate that a person's heart attitude is a factor in God honoring a person's faith? One thing is for sure: faith, even from a most unworthy person's prayer, opens the door for Jesus to help.

The second person, a woman who Jesus said had *great faith*, was also non-Jewish. She pleaded for Jesus to come and heal her daughter of demon possession (Matthew 15:21-28). He told her, "I was sent only to the lost sheep of the house of Israel." Not put off, she bowed down before him and said, "Lord help me!" Again, Jesus put her off by saying, "It is not good to take the children's bread and throw it to the dogs." "Yes, Lord," she said, "but even the dogs feed on the crumbs which fall from their masters' table." Jesus responded, "O woman, *your faith is great*; it shall be done for you as you wish." We might say that great faith persists until receiving an answer. However, her persistence was not the major factor. She believed Jesus was her master, and she knew he cared about people from all nations. Her great faith was based on her undying conviction that Jesus's love for her would not fail.

Strong faith is contrasted with weak faith in Romans 4:18-22. When Abraham faced seemingly impossible situations and was given a promise from God, he had a choice to believe God's promise or not. Strong faith means we are fully assured, without any wavering, that what God promises he is able to perform. This applies to us as well as to Abraham. For example, at times in my life I have doubted that God could forgive all the wrongs I have done, thinking I was not worthy of being forgiven. I had weak faith. I have strong faith when I believe God has forgiven all my sin. Strong faith is fully assured that God's promise of forgiveness is certain (Romans 4:5-8). Strong faith unwaveringly trusts God and believes all God's promises in scripture, including our future bodily resurrection from the dead (1 Corinthians 6:14) and our future inheritance of the world (Romans 4:13).

SELF-EXAMINATION

The above descriptions of faith help us think about our own faith. According to the following scriptures, God encourages self-examination. "Search me, O God, and know my heart" (Psalm 139:23). "Let us examine and probe our ways" (Lamentations 3:40). "Test yourselves to see if you are in *the faith*; examine yourselves!" (2 Corinthians 13:5).

Considering what you've read in this chapter, how would you answer these three questions: (1) What is the object of my faith? (2) What does my faith guarantee? Is it trustworthy? Why do I believe it? (3) To what degree do I trust God and his Word? What specific actions show that I have faith? For example, I fear flying in planes. Recently, I flew, believing it's OK if the plane crashes, for I would be with the Lord. I experienced peace. And thanks be to God, for it was God's grace that he gave me peace (John 14:27).

CHAPTER 4

HOW FAITH IN CHRIST HELPS TO BREAK ADDICTIONS

People in churches can be very judgmental or prejudiced against those caught in the web of sinful behaviors and habits. Self-righteousness does little to help those who need the love and new life that Jesus Christ offers. Here is an example of a life-giving church. One of their members came and asked for help regarding a spouse who had a life-dominating problem that was destroying their home. The church investigated the problem, gathered money to pay for the person to go to a treatment center, mailed the person cards and notes of encouragement, and welcomed the person back home with a promise of continued moral support. What a great model of the love of Christ in action. Of course, people who are not followers of Christ can do the same kinds of things, but followers of Jesus should do no less.

A life-dominating problem is one that is controlling and ruining a person's life and is seemingly impossible to overcome. The drug user, or gambler, or alcoholic, or sex abuser, or pornography addict, or overeater, or whoever else with whatever else, cannot stop their habit, even though it is wrecking their life and the lives of others.

Some, with pressure, or who finally gain a bit of sanity, agree to enter a program to get help. With great effort, they learn to rely on others, achieve some success at overcoming, and hope they are able to restore all, or part, of what they have lost. All of us struggle with something that we feel is constantly defeating us. Christians are not exempt, for we are all sinners and our sinful nature is powerful.

For those unfamiliar with biblical terminology, our "sinful nature" means our corrupted human nature trapped in destructive thinking and behaviors. For example, there is a list of sinful behaviors in Mark 7:21-23, Galatians 5:19-21, and 2 Timothy 3:1-5. Some who proclaim the gospel of Christ say that if you accept Jesus into your life, he will take away your problem. This does happen with some people, but with many, it does not. In cases where it does not, those persons may conclude that trying the "Jesus way" did not work for them, and so they walk away from him. What they fail to understand, perhaps because they have not had the opportunity to learn it, is that Christ did not come to help us change our corrupt human nature but to destroy it altogether and replace it with a new nature and a new way of life (Ezekiel 11:19-20; 36:25-27; John 3:6-8; 2 Corinthians 5:17; Galatians 2:20).

Have you considered what being a new creation in Christ means? You are no longer your old self, the one who has no power over sin. You now have a divine nature, which has been implanted within you (2 Peter 1:3-4), and the goal is to learn to live as your new self (Colossians 3:9-10). Rather than think we can change our old sinful nature, we learn to walk in the Spirit and experience behaviors that come from the Spirit, not from our old self. We can never change our corrupted nature; we can only discipline and subdue it as we learn to live by the Spirit (1 Corinthians 9:27). Admittedly, we may fluctuate back and forth between the sinful self and the Spirit-led self, but our goal is to learn to walk in the Spirit more than in our sinful nature.

However, when we do yield to our bad self, we must remember that this part of us has died with Christ on the cross and is not really who we are (Romans 6:6). We are the new self and that is where we put our focus. Success over life-dominating problems comes when we rely on the new spiritual dynamics that Jesus introduces into our lives. We believers in Christ are called to walk with Christ and to live like Christ would want (Ephesians 5:1-2). He came to save us from our sins so that they would not continue to destroy us, nor our fellowship with God, nor our relationships with others.

Continuing in wrong habitual patterns causes our lives to deteriorate in many ways. These habits personally affect us physically, mentally, emotionally, spiritually, and socially. I could go into detail to show how self-destruction works, but if you are struggling with bad habits, you already know this. The Bible is very clear that sin leads to death (Romans 6:23), not just physically but in every other way. We know this, not only because God's Word says it but because we experience it. When we are unable to overcome our weaknesses, we can have a hard time living with ourselves, God, and others. Sinful habits are difficult to overcome. Although some can claim to have been "delivered" from a habit when Christ entered into their lives, many others must fight to win (Galatians 5:17). Furthermore, if we often lose the fight, it is easy to get tired of fighting and to give in. It is good to pursue grace from God and to ask him to deliver us from our curse, for with God, deliverance is a real possibility. However, in this chapter, I want to address those fellow strugglers who have not been able to experience such deliverance (Romans 7:24).

How does faith in Christ help to provide the answer we need for overcoming our problematic habit? Two fundamental necessities must be in place to be able to overcome a sinful habit. First, the determination to never give in to the habit (1 Corinthians 9:24-27; 2 Timothy 4:7), and second, being free from guilt and from feelings of guilt and shame so that we do not berate or beat ourselves up and lose the battle by getting discouraged and depressed (Romans 8:1-2). Following is a fuller explanation of these two necessities for winning.

FAITH NEVER QUITS

First, never quit. In twenty years of doing fifth-step counseling at an alcoholic treatment center, I heard this often-used phrase from those battling alcohol: "If you fall and get up every time, you are not a loser." What motivates a believer in Christ to never quit? The necessary motivation begins with a conversion experience. This means to become a new creation in Christ. Jesus called it by different names, such as "being born again," "being born of the Spirit," "drinking the living water I will give," "being saved," or "turning from darkness to light" (John 3:3-6; 4:13-14; 7:37-39; Acts 2:38-40; 26:16-18). The first three steps in Alcoholics Anonymous declare this need for conversion by saying that we must admit our powerlessness to overcome our habit, recognize there is a God who can save us, and turn our will and life over to the care of that God. When we trust Jesus as our higher power, ask him to save us, and have faith that he will, God does a miracle in our lives. He puts within us his Holy Spirit who creates in us a new life (Ezekiel 11:19-20; Romans 8:9; Ephesians 1:13-14).

This gift of new life in you provides true motivation never to quit. God's mercy and presence in us causes us to think things like, *I hate this sin, and I will not give in and let it destroy me* (Proverbs 8:13). When we hate something, especially something God hates and something that is destroying our lives, we are more motivated to take steps to avoid it. Another thought may be, *He loves me, and he suffered and gave up his life so I could experience his forgiveness. I love God and I want to please him* (1 John 5:3). Love is a great motivator. We tend to want to love and please those who deeply love us. One other thought we may have is, *God wants me to be holy as he is holy; and I want that* (1 Peter 1:14-16). When we know that we are God's children and are destined one day to be like Jesus, such hope strongly motivates us to purify ourselves, just as he is pure (1 John 3:2-3).

In our newly motivated determination never to give up, we look for any Spirit-led method to try that will work for us (Romans 6:12-13). It may be finding a person or group to hold us accountable, memorizing and often repeating parts of God's Word, forming a plan to avoid tempting situations, or learning to rid ourselves of initial thoughts that start us down the road to defeat. It may be learning to quit trying so hard and to rest in God's provisions, not focusing on the habit but focusing on a positive life of prayer, loving others by practicing good deeds, or enjoying life's fun activities and developing a hobby. We decide, and re-decide, to become willing to try to do whatever it takes, trusting God to help us. A method my friend uses that works for him is that he made a commitment never to keep a secret. He has someone with whom he tells any thoughts or actions that he might be tempted to keep secret, particularly those things having to do with a problem area he is seeking to overcome (James 5:16).

The Bible gives us practical guidance on things we can do to overcome a habit. Consider these examples. "Do not be conformed to this world, but be transformed by the renewing of your mind" (Romans 12:2). "Put on the Lord Jesus Christ, and make no provision for the flesh in regard to its lusts" (Romans 13:14). "Do not be deceived: bad company corrupts good morals" (1 Corinthians 15:33). Learning what statements like these mean and using your imagination to figure out how you can practice them can help. No matter what methods we try, we need always to be praying for God to help us and show us what will work for us. Different things work for different people.

Something that has helped me when I feel discouraged is to see a broader perspective about my life. I can easily look at the negative aspects of my life and let those be my focus. But my bad habits are not the things that define my life. There is much more to my life than that. Look at all the good and positive things. Jesus said that no one can serve two masters (Matthew 6:24). We need to stop letting our habits be our master, and let Jesus be our master. We need to focus on what he says about us and on living for Christ—doing his work and engaging in the kind of lifestyle he is teaching and leading us to practice.

As we get involved in thinking about others and caring for other people by serving their needs, we feel better about ourselves and our motivation never to quit improves. We do not have time to focus on our negatives, and we see progress. We enjoy the life God is giving us. Our faith in Christ's salvation teaches us to say, "My sin is not who I am" (Romans 7:17, 20; 1 Corinthians 6:9-11). Continually believing and affirming who I am in Christ is what defines who I really am. The ability to have this positive perspective produces a kind of freedom that goes a long way in helping us overcome evils that are trying to destroy us.

FAITH FREES US FROM GUILT AND SHAME

The second necessity for overcoming a sinful, life-dominating habit is to be free of guilt, including guilt feelings and feelings of shame. Without this, we get tired of our sin and we feel hopeless and think, *What's the use?* We give in to the sin and we give up believing we can ever be the kind of person Christ is helping us to become. The spirit of Satan will often be around to accuse us of not being a good Christ-follower (Revelation 12:9-10). If an inner voice tells you that you cannot be a true Christian since you keep living like you do, don't listen to those thoughts. Counter them with the truth. *I am in Christ, and he is in me. He loves me. He accepts me. This sin does not drive Jesus away from me. He will never desert me but is planning to bring me into his eternal kingdom* (Romans 8:1; 1 John 3:1-2; Philippians 1:6; 2 Timothy 4:18).

How does one gain freedom from guilt and shameful feelings? Every time, every time, every time, every time I repeat the same wrong, I pray something like, "Father in heaven, I have blown it again. How can I love you and hurt you like this? I hate this sin. Thank you for sending Christ to me. Thank you that he paid for my sin. Thank you that I am forgiven. Thank you that you still love and accept me. I want to do better. Help me to live a life pleasing to you. You deserve my best." Then I get up again, believe his forgiveness, and walk on without guilt and shame but with determination to live right. I re-engage in whatever I can do to not quit.

Faith in Christ means I never stop believing his love and forgiveness. His cross took away my sin and shame forever (1 Peter 2:24). Every time I mess up, I again exercise my faith in his forgiveness. It is like having an ongoing, never-ending new start. The temptation is to think that since it is easy to get God's forgiveness, I can stop trying to be rid of the sin; after all, God will forgive me. This is where we must remind ourselves not to let this sin continue. I must still fight the battle, but I can do it more successfully without guilt, beating up myself, and thinking I am a failure.

Eventually, this cycle of failure and faith in forgiveness, failure and faith in forgiveness, begins to break me down. How can he keep forgiving me? I may weep when I realize how much God loves me. That he keeps forgiving me no matter how many times I fail and sincerely confess it is an overwhelming thought (1 John 1:9). I may feel bad that I fail him but never that I am a bad person, for he understands and accepts me. I begin to accept that I am a new person in Christ and that my sin does not define me. I believe that I am of great worth to God. He went to the cross for me, and he is transforming me (2 Corinthians 3:18; 4:16-18).

This kind of faith thinking motivates me even more to ask and trust him to help me live a better life. I come away from such humbled times with God renewed and happy, but also saying, "I cannot keep doing this sin; I must find a way to stop" (John 8:10-11). When guilt and shame are never allowed to weigh me down and make me depressed, I have renewed energy and a reason to live and to keep pursuing my walk with Christ. I resume living for him. I resume my daily life, with its "normal" activities, stresses, and good times. Forget the sin you just committed again. God has forgiven and removed it from his sight. So must you (Psalm 103:1-5, 12-14). Press on. Concentrate on the good life he is giving you and on your future hope in Christ. If it is hard to believe that God loves you, it may be helpful for you to be around loving Christian friends who can affirm their love for you. This will help you believe God's love (Proverbs 27:17).

Do you need confirmation from the Bible of what I have been saying? If so, I recommend reading and meditating on Romans 6–8. In summary, faith in Christ helps a person overcome sinful habits and succeed in new ones, by providing two necessities. First is the spiritual motivation to never give up fighting the good fight to live the Christ life (2 Timothy 4:7). Second, freedom from guilt and shameful feelings comes by believing Christ's forgiveness and loving acceptance every time sin happens (Romans 8:1). May the grace, peace, and victory of Christ Jesus be with you.

CHAPTER 5

FAITH AND SELF-IDENTITY

W e all see ourselves in different ways—some positive, some negative, and some a mixture of both. Ask people how they would describe themselves and you get as many answers as there are people. Well, maybe not. I'm sure we could find groupings of people with similar traits, although I am convinced that no two people are totally alike. It is undoubtedly safe to say that no one knows him or herself completely; some know themselves better than others do, some have very little idea of who they are, and perhaps some do not want to know. How people see themselves determines how they live their lives; therefore, a good and positive self-image is very important.

Certainly, the American culture is concerned about helping people build positive self-images. Teachers in elementary schools recognize that kids who have positive self-images do better in life than those who do not. I participated in my community's public school system at a time when they purchased an elementary through high school curriculum, specifically designed to help build a positive self-image in each child. They realized its importance. Most are probably unaware that the God of the Judeo-Christian faith is concerned about doing the same, for he tells us to build one another up (1 Thessalonians 5:11; Ephesians 4:29). God created humans in his image and declared them good. However, in their going away from God, they severely marred and lost his likeness in them. God has a plan to restore people to his likeness, and that is the subject of this chapter. But we must first be able to see our problem.

Here is an example of a person whose self-identity is in ruin. God's goodness in them has been invaded by evil. The person is unstable because there is within them a conflict between their good self and their evil self. Such a person is struggling to achieve a proper self-identity. On the one side, the person has come to see him or herself as worthless and no good. It may have been that in younger days, the person was abused physically or mentally, or was abandoned by someone they trusted to protect them, or was forced to obey strict rules and was severely punished when he or she messed up. Perhaps this person constantly received the message that he or she would never amount to anything and was a bad person.

Is it any wonder that such a person grows up feeling unloved and unwanted? They may live in anger, fear of rejection, shame, self-pity, self-blame, or guilt. They are constantly reminded of their failures and worthlessness whenever something goes wrong or something bad happens to them. Eventually, believing they are no good, they may feel they don't deserve another's love and help. Or, if someone does care about them, they run away from it for fear they will be rejected and hurt again.

The other side of this person is one that strives to be good so they feel worthy of acceptance and love. By caring about others and doing good things for others, they try to earn others' love and respect. If they can achieve success, gain riches or popularity, or be helpful to people around them, they feel good about themselves, and this is the identity they take on to cancel out their other side.

Religion is also something they try to incorporate into their lives, believing that if they can follow religious commands and practice religious teachings, God and others will love and accept them. Unfortunately, their attempts at being good do not work, for the evil without and within them make it impossible to be consistently good all the time, and any failure sends them back to their worthless side again. They may try to hang on to their faith in religion, but God does not seem to be helping them, largely because they misunderstand what an "in Christ" identity is all about, and their religion is nothing more than a self-effort to make life work. They are trying to save themselves to prove to themselves and others that they are somebody of worth. Not being able to make life work, and entertaining a feeling of hopelessness, they often turn to things that will make themselves feel better—things like alcohol, porn, work, games, drugs, crime, or whatever it may be that allows them to escape their pain.

Even if they should become successful in life, the unworthy side is always with them, and they still feel empty because success and money cannot buy the love they seek. Love is not something to be earned; otherwise, being loved would always depend on their performance, as they think that *others will love me if I . . .*, or *because I . . . .* We are imperfect people, and love earned by performance is not the kind of love we need. How does one, then, escape this cycle of, *I am no good . . . I am good . . . I am no good . . . I am good?* Such a self-identity is two people in a cyclical struggle to find acceptance, love, and worthiness, and the cycle seems endless and often discouraging, depressing, and hopeless. This double-minded self-identity results in an unstable life. Can one ever get out of it? How does a person get beyond a crippling human self-identity and discover a needed new identity?

Jesus told a story of two lost sons in need of love (read Luke 15:11-32). The father loved his two sons very much. In fact, his love for them was perfect and unending. Unfortunately, due to ignorance, neither son realized his father's love. They did not know that contentment, happiness, peace, freedom, and the enjoyment of pleasures came from knowing and possessing the love of their father.

One son, feeling restless and too restrained, decided to leave the father and journey out to experience greater freedom. He thought freedom was doing what he wanted to do. He pursued the life he thought would make him happy, but all did not go as he planned. He did not have what it took to overcome the evils both within himself and in the world. His own passions enslaved him, he ran into troubles due to failed relationships, and he began to struggle to make life work. Eventually, his resources diminished, and what others did to help him failed to satisfy a deep hunger for the life he hoped to find.

One day, this son awoke to the fact that his life was in ruin and he had nothing left, not even his dignity and sense of self-worth. He thought about his father, thinking that life with his father had to be better than the life he was living. He decided to go home and admit he was wrong for believing that doing his own thing, apart from the father, was a better way to live. Although feeling shame and unsure of his father's response, he would humbly ask his father if he could come back.

As he neared home, with unexpected astonishment the son felt overwhelmed by the non-judgmental warmth and eager love of his father. Realizing his son's change of heart, the father ordered a great celebration in honor of his return. I suspect that the love he experienced from his father caused his father's kind of love to be born in his own heart, and through that love, he discovered and lived the kind of life that went way beyond what he ever imagined could be possible.

The other son, even though he religiously stayed with the father, was likewise ignorant of the father's love. When he saw how his father loved his disgraceful brother, he was angry and did not attend the welcome home party. If he had truly known the love of the father, he would have loved his brother. To him, love was something to be earned by being good and obeying the father's wishes. His brother did not deserve to be loved but to be reprimanded and punished for his shameful, unruly, and delinquent lifestyle.

When the stay-at-home son did not listen to his father's plea to come to the party, he proved to be as guilty of mismanaging life as his brother. In truth, he deserved judgment for his self-righteousness and his refusal to understand what love was all about. I suspect that this son, if never coming to know the father's lovingkindness, would have a long-standing resentment toward his brother, never allowing him to regain an honorable love and respect.

Jesus's telling of this story lets us know that finding love is difficult, for we are ignorant of what love is. The father of the story represents the God who made us, whose love is pure, endless, and unadulterated. We don't find love by trying to live our own life away from the love of the father, nor do we find love by trying to do the impossible and be good enough to earn it. We find love when we experience God's undeserved acceptance and have his love instilled in us by his Spirit. We find love when we continually trust the Father's love toward us, especially in times we mess up (1 John 4:16). Love happens through our relationship with the father and by learning, with the encouraging company of fellow believers, to practice the same kind of love that God has given us.

To experience the love we need and desire, we must experience God's love and come to be at peace with him. The lost son shows us what is needed on our part. Another story Jesus told shows us the same thing (read Luke 18:9-14). By our own misguided thinking and actions, we have distanced ourselves from God, and this must be overcome. Love, oneness, and peace with God takes place when we realize how God loved us in Christ. "God demonstrates his love toward us, in that while we were yet sinners, Christ died for us" (Romans 5:8). This realization humbles us and causes us to repent of our errant ways. The wrongs we have done need to be erased so that they are no longer part of our identity. This happens when God, whose love requires him to be a just and holy God, declares us not guilty and frees us from any need for punishment. Most people do not know that God has justly done this for us based on Jesus's death. This gift of God's love and forgiveness results in a new identity for us.

You've probably heard of the twelve steps used by alcoholics, and others, to help them achieve freedom from their addictions. The first three steps are what Jesus is telling us to do if we want to rid ourselves of the past and discover a new identity. Allow me to paraphrase them.

Step one: We admit we are powerless over our dysfunctional thoughts and behaviors—that our lives have become unmanageable. I might add that we must admit our powerlessness, by our self-efforts or self-righteousness, to get from others the kind of love and acceptance we need.

Step two: We come to believe that God, a power greater than ourselves, can restore us to sanity and stability. I add that God wants to restore us to a life of love and great worth.

Step three: We make a decision to turn our will and our lives over to the care of God (not as we understand him but as he reveals himself in the Bible). Turning our life over to God does not mean that we lose our freedom of will, but that we become willing to accept what God's will is for our lives. His will is that we humble ourselves and, by faith, receive his gifts of forgiveness, new life, and his Holy Spirit of love. When that happens, we will be empowered to know and experience a new identity in Christ, one that is freed from those things that have enslaved us. Christianity is a relationship to be entered into and developed. It is a life of faith, trusting God for what we cannot do.

Jesus asked a man who had been sick for thirty-eight years, "Do you wish to get well?" (John 5:2-15). It seems like a foolish or unwarranted question. Of course he wants to get well; he's been sick for many years. Ray Stedman (1917–1992), a respected pastor, once said something about this passage that caused me to realize the importance of the question. He said, "What a strange question to ask of a man who had been sick for thirty-eight years!" Actually, it's a very good question to discover where people are who are asking for help. It is very difficult, if not impossible, to help someone who does not want help. It is surprising to come across people who are sick with diseases, mental or emotional issues, marital problems, or life-dominating addictions, and who do not want help, even though they appear to want it. The help they want must be on their own terms, and if not, they reject it.

People do not want to get well for any number of reasons. People caught up in destructive immoral practices such as porn or adultery, or habits like alcohol or drugs, do not want to get well because they do not want to give up the pleasure or comfort they get from what they are doing. Some do not want to get well because they fear failure and letting people down. Some do not want to get well because they want the sympathy, attention, and help they get from others who feel sorry for them. Some don't want change, fearing the unknown or having feelings of insecurity. Some won't get well because they are too proud to admit weakness and accept help. Some will not get well because they think they can do it themselves in their own way. Some won't get well because they do not think they deserve it, and they think that punishing themselves makes up for their guilt. Some have already given up hope for change, and nothing can convince them that help is possible. Many lack the faith to believe God can help them. Humans can be their own worst enemies when it comes to getting well.

Returning to the story of the sick man, when Jesus asked the man if he wanted to get well, the man answered that he needed someone to help him. What Jesus told him to do was different than he expected. To try to do what Jesus wanted him to do would take a great measure of faith, for what Jesus told him was seemingly impossible. No way could he do it himself. He must believe in a power greater than himself that could restore him, and he must trust Jesus and do what he was told. Jesus told him to "get up, pick up his mat, and walk." Immediately, and amazingly, the man stood up, picked up his pallet, and walked (John 5:8-9). Even if his faith was weak, his own way had never worked. What did he have to lose? So why not try Jesus's way?

When he took that step of faith in Jesus and his word, a miracle happened. He was no longer tied to his old identity. Everyone else had ignored him, putting themselves first. No one else had the power to save him and make him whole. He was a man loved by someone who cared. He could now do things he could not do before. Jesus became his number one reason for living, for to Jesus he owed his life. Jesus gave him a new identity. He would now walk a new path, the one Jesus would teach him. He would now live like the Apostle Paul who said, "I have been crucified with Christ; and it is no longer I who live, but Christ lives in me; and the life which I now live in the flesh I live by faith in the Son of God, who loved me and gave Himself up for me" (Galatians 2:20). To be healed of our crippling identity, we need to trust Jesus and do what he says. When we do that, we acquire a new and different identity. We will still possess two identities, the old and the new, but if we remember who we are in Christ, we will have new motivation and power to conquer the things that work to destroy us.

In one of Paul's letters, he wrote about our self-identity when he said, "The flesh sets its desire against the Spirit, and the Spirit against the flesh; for they are in opposition to one another"

(Galatians 5:17). Christians have two identities. We still have our former fleshly identity, and now we have a new spiritual identity. We must die to our old identity and live in our new identity. We cannot live a healthy life, trying to be in two worlds at the same time, carrying two identities that conflict with each other. The Bible says, "A double-minded man [is] unstable in all his ways" (James 1:8). Jesus warned that any kingdom, city, or house divided against itself cannot stand (Matthew 12:25).

As Christians, there is an ongoing battle within us to determine which identity controls us. Will it be our fleshly identity or our "in Christ" identity? The Bible says we can be a new creation in Christ Jesus; the old is passed away and the new has come (2 Corinthians 5:17). In Christ, we have a positive and glorious self-image when we learn to see ourselves as God sees us. In order to experience wholeness and well-being and to have the ability to meet the needs of others, it is very important to understand what God says about who we are in Christ.

Remember, for the man who was sick for thirty-eight years and was told to do what seemed impossible, Jesus was able to make the impossible happen. The lost son was at odds with his father. He realized he had sinned against his father and that if he was to enter his father's world again, he must be made right with his father. He does what Jesus said to do: "Repent and believe in God's good news" (Mark 1:14-15). How is it that the father could love the son and so quickly forgive and welcome him home? It is because the father had already forgiven the son, though the son did not know it. The father in this story can represent our heavenly Father. God the Father forgives us before we know it because he has already made provision for his forgiveness through the death of his Son, Jesus. What Jesus did made it possible for us to be right with God, to be restored to the likeness of God, and to be made perfect in God's sight. What Jesus did was an act of God's love (Romans 5:8), and it gives us the opportunity for the miracle of new life and a new identity to happen.

Through faith in God and his word, we too become righteous, justified before God, declared not guilty, reconciled to him, and at peace with God. Christ, through his selfless act of love on our behalf, has become our means of righteousness (Philippians 3:7-11). In him by faith, we are loved by God, forgiven, and the children of God (John 1:12-13; 3:3-8; 1 John 3:1-2; 4:16). Furthermore, we have received God's promise of the Holy Spirit (Ephesians 1:13-14), which is the miracle that causes us to be born of God and convinces us of God's love (Romans 5:5; 8:9-10, 15-17). It is important to be reminded again and again that in Christ we are righteous, forgiven, loved, and a child of God. Our new identity is now in him.

What is meant by identity in Christ? We are not who we think we are or who others say we are; it is who God our Father, and Jesus, says we are. Instead of letting our past define us, instead of believing the names others have called us, we believe what the Bible calls us. Consider something the Apostle Paul said concerning himself. He said, "If I am doing the very thing I do not want, I am no longer the one doing it, but sin which dwells in me" (Romans 7:20). I read this once and thought, *Is Paul a schizophrenic, or what? When I sin, I think I did it, but when Paul sins, he thinks it wasn't him doing it.* I believe Paul is acknowledging that sin was part of his old life, but he has now reckoned that part of his life to be dead. He no longer sees himself as a worthless person full of sinfulness. He does not want that life anymore. He sees himself as a new person with a new life, and he now lives the life Jesus wants him to live. In letters Paul wrote, he encourages believers to set aside the old self and put on the new self (Ephesians 4:22-24; Colossians 3:9-10; Romans 6:1-13).

Following are a few Bible verses that tell us who we are and what we have "in Christ." Whenever self-condemning thoughts or feelings of worthlessness enter your mind, counter them with what God says about you. The chapter in this book titled "Fight the Good Fight of Faith" will help you know how to do this by using the shield of faith and the sword of the Spirit. In the scriptures below, what does God say about you? Perhaps you could make a list, pick out some that are particularly applicable to you, and pray often that God would help you believe what he says.

- Psalm 103:10-14

- Matthew 6:25-26

- John 8:12; 10:27-28; 11:25-26

- Romans 4:3-5; 5:1, 11; 7:4; 8:1; 8:28-39
- 1 Corinthians 6:9-11; 19-20; 15:51-57
- 2 Corinthians 5:15, 21
- Galatians 4:6-7; 5:13
- Ephesians 1:7; 2:10; 2:19-22
- Philippians 3:20-21
- Colossians 1:13-14; 3:9-10, 12
- 1 Thessalonians 4:9
- Hebrews 10:39
- 1 Peter 1:3, 5; 2:9-10; 5:7
- 2 Peter 1:3-4
- 1 John 2:1-2; 3:1-3; 4:15-16
- Revelation 5:9-10; 12:9-11

CHAPTER 6

FIGHT THE
GOOD FIGHT OF FAITH

(. . . using the shield of faith and the sword of the Spirit)

You may be one of millions who bought a George Foreman grill. But how many know about George Foreman, an Olympic gold medalist, world champion heavyweight boxer, and surprisingly, a professing believer in Jesus and a minister of the faith? After losing his title to Muhammad Ali in the early 70s, and after being out of boxing for twenty years, he returned at age forty-five to regain his title with an unexpected upset win over a much younger opponent. How did he do it? It certainly took disciplined workouts to get into shape, but beyond that, Foreman overcame the odds against him by having a plan on how to knock out his opposition with a powerful punch that he dreamt would work.

In the sport of boxing, the goal is to knock the opponent down and out and protect yourself so the other can't do it to you. The Apostle Paul mentions boxing in the Bible and makes the point that the goal in any sport is to win (1 Corinthians 9:24-27). In a tough world where we face many opposing forces that threaten to knock us out, it is not easy to win. We must fight the good fight (1 Timothy 6:12; 2 Timothy 4:7). To survive the forces that threaten our faith, we need discipline, a plan, and a powerful punch—like George Foreman.

FIVE STORIES

(A Bible study for individuals or groups about our fight for faith.)

What threatens to destroy one's faith? As you read each story, answer the questions below to discover what the stories say and teach about fighting the good fight. Passages in the parentheses provide additional information to think about that could aid in answering the questions.

1. Adam and Eve's Story—Genesis 3:1-13 (1 John 2:15-17)

2. Jesus's Story—Luke 4:1-13 (Luke 2:42-52; 3:21-22)

3. Job's Story—Job 1:1-22; 2:1-13; 3:11, 25-26; 10:7-8; 19:25-27; 38:1-7; 40:1-14; 42:1-6, 10-12

4. The Israelites' Story—1 Corinthians 10:1-13; Psalm 78:9-33; Exodus 16:2-4; 17:1-7; 32:1-10; Numbers 25:1-3 (James 1:13-15)

5. The Apostle Paul's Story—2 Timothy 4:6-8 (Acts 9:1-22; 1 Corinthians 4:11-13; 2 Corinthians 11:24-29; 1:8-11; Philippians 4:11-13; 1 Timothy 6:6-12; Philippians 3:7-11)

The Questions

1. Before the person (or persons) was tempted, what was his or her relationship with God like?

2. Who or what is tempting whom, and what battles are taking place, internally and without?

3. What happened to cause the tempted one(s) to win or lose the fight?

4. During the battle, did the tempted one(s) consult with God on what to say or do?

5. Based on your study, what have you learned that could help you in your fight?

The Enemy

Christians believe there is one opponent particularly adept at defeating us (1 Peter 5:8). He knocked Adam and Eve down and out during the very beginnings of human life, thus opening the door for evil to enter our world (Genesis 3:1-13). Since then, having become more self-centered than God-centered, we become easy prey to the dangers and distractions of this world. We have become a fallen race and victims to such things as fear, drug addictions, pornography, sexual misconduct, love of money, materialism, worldly pleasures, good-sounding but false philosophies, angry and hateful words and behaviors, violence, death, and on and on. Satan remains our enemy, using our human weaknesses, our bent toward self-will, our inner lustful desires, and the things offered by this world to tempt us away from our Creator and into self-seeking fulfillment. This leads to damaged lives, emptiness, unhappiness, and us becoming tools for the destruction of self and others.

You may think such a being who is the enemy of our souls does not exist.[8] However, even if you cannot believe a devil exists, few deny that the world is full of temptations and evil forces that cause our lives to take a wrong turn, ruining our peace and well-being. Jesus described the devil as a murderer who speaks lies to get us to believe things that are not true (John 8:44). "You don't need God," the devil says. "You can be your own person and have a good life without him." Satan can appear as an angel of light—that is, his deceptive messages can seem to us to be right and good (2 Corinthians 11:14; Proverbs 14:12).

Satan tried to get Jesus to listen to him instead of to God, tempting him to doubt himself and take steps to prove he was the Son of God. Furthermore, Satan tempted him to go after the power and riches of this world instead of living out God's purposes. He even tempted Jesus to use his Jewish scriptural truths in a way that

---

8. Psychiatrist M. Scott Peck wrote a nationwide best seller, *People of the Lie: The Hope for Healing Human Evil* (New York: Simon and Schuster, 1983). The author explains how he came to believe in the existence of a devil. He also states that evil deeds do not make an evil person and goes on to define what causes evil in people and how to overcome it. This fascinating book will hold your attention, unless, of course, you are an evil person, for evil people are those who continue to believe the lie.

would make God his servant instead of the master. Jesus did not fall for Satan's deceptive attempts to knock him out (Luke 4:1-13; Matthew 4:1-11). In fact, the Bible says Jesus came into the world to destroy the works of the devil (1 John 3:8). Jesus tells his followers to take courage, for he has overcome any opposition the world can throw against us (John 16:33). We need not fear or give in to enemy attacks, for the Bible says, "Greater is He who is in you than he who is in the world," and "The victory that has overcome the world [is] our faith" (1 John 4:4; 5:4). Though the devil seeks to devour us, God gives us what we need to guarantee our victory. Our task is to resist the adversary, stand firm in faith, and rely on the gracious help of God to help us overcome (1 Peter 5:8-10).

HOW WE FIGHT

Paul uses the analogy of ancient warfare (Ephesians 6:11-13). Military terms are used to describe the armor of God that we must use to win the fight over enemies that would destroy us. A soldier would use his shield to protect himself from the life-destroying weapons of the enemy. At the same time, the sword was used to attack the enemy and gain victory over him (Ephesians 6:16-17). The Bible presents a picture of Satan shooting arrows or darts at us. Satan uses half-truths to make his lies sound good—words that include both *good* and *evil*. God, however, cannot lie (Titus 1:2). He always tells the truth. God's Word is truth. Jesus said that the truth is what sets us free (John 8:32). When discouraging, depressing, negative, and ungodly thoughts enter my mind, I take them as harmful missiles that are either from the devil, from others, or from my old depraved self, and God encourages me to fight by taking up the shield of faith and the sword of the Spirit, which is the Word of God. We must use these weapons and do as Paul said to Timothy: "Fight the good fight of faith" (1 Timothy 6:12).

How, then, can we build a shield of faith and use the sword of the Spirit? The best way we can begin building a shield of faith is to ask the Lord to help us identify disturbing, negative, critical, or depressing thoughts that come to mind and the situations that bring them on. The shield is *recognizing* the thoughts, words, and feelings that want to come into our heart and mind and control us. The shield then *recalls* the words of God that need to be held up to block the words that are trying to defeat us. The sooner I can recognize such thoughts or feelings that are entering my mind, the easier it is to ward them off.

The sword is what I say inwardly or aloud to get them to leave. Like Jesus did, I am to use the sword of the Spirit, which is the Word of God, as an offensive weapon to knock out those damaging thoughts. Each time the bad thought or emotion occurs, I repeat the words until my faith in God's truths calms me and gets what is bothering me to leave; at least, that's the goal. This clears the way for us to have the mind of Christ direct us in how God would have us think and live (1 Corinthians 2:15-16). Therefore, to fight Satan's evil lies, we tell the truth of how we feel, the truth of what we've done, and the truth of God's Word. Following are some examples.

> **Voice**: "You are no good, you're worthless, you are a bad person."
>
> **God's Truth**: "That's not true! I am a child of God, my Father. He loves and cares about me, and I am of great worth to him" (Matthew 6:26).

> **Voice**: "You can't be a Christian; you can't be a child of God. You just blew it and sinned again." (Satan frequently tries to bring up our past or present sins— Revelation 12:10-11.)
>
> **God's Truth**: "Jesus took my sin, past and present, in his body on the cross, and suffered my death. You are right, I am guilty, but I honestly confessed my wrongs to God. He has forgiven me, and I want to live his way and not mine. I have died to my old self, and now I choose to follow my new self in Christ" (1 Peter 2:24-25; 1 John 1:9; Psalm 32:5; Ephesians 4:20-24).

Voice: "You got angry again—you're selfish. Forget about trying to be good. You can't do it."

God's Truth: "I'm sorry I failed you, Lord. Thank you for forgiving me because of what Jesus did on the cross. Help me not to repeat this and to do better." (As believers, we move forward without guilt, avoiding the trap of condemnation. This frees us to work at being better with the help of God and others. We are able to fight the good fight when we do not let ourselves fall into the guilt trap [Romans 8:1].)

Voice: "You can't believe God's Word about loving you is true. You don't feel loved, do you? No! You know you are not worthy of his love."

God's Truth: "My belief that I am God's beloved child is not based on my feelings. God's Word is true. He says he loves me, and God does not lie. I believe his Word, not my feelings" (1 John 3:1).

Voice: "All this stuff about God and Jesus is not true. The Bible is just a bunch of made-up stories and myths."

God's Truth: "The fact that Jesus lived, died, and rose again is true. Evidence that the testimonies of those eyewitnesses who saw these things and wrote about them is beyond reasonable doubt. Be gone, Satan. I believe and know that what those people saw and heard is true" (2 Peter 1:16-18; 1 John 1:1-4).

Voice: "Go ahead, do what you feel like and want to do. Even though you know it's wrong, God will forgive you."

God's Truth: "Go away, Devil! This is wrong, and I will run from it. I choose to live God's way. It is right and best for me and others." (We need to get rid of tempting thoughts the moment they enter our minds. Think about something else, or run somewhere else. The reason we choose not to sin is because we are a new person in Christ and we want to please him for saving us—Romans 6:1-7, 11-13, 20-23.)

Voice: (Someone wronged and hurt you, and anger wells up inside you:) "That person wronged and hurt you; they don't deserve forgiveness. They must pay for their wrongs. Give them what they deserve and teach them a lesson."

God's Truth: "'"Vengeance is mine; I will repay," says the Lord.' Practice loving your enemies. Do good, and pray for them. Turn them over to me and trust my justice will come on them in my time." (Do what you can to be at peace, but you do not have to keep letting them hurt you. If you are in a continuous relationship with them, needed change must be pursued for the good of all involved. If crime is committed, you can turn the person over to the proper authorities for the protection of self and others. That would be the loving thing to do. [See Romans 12:17-21; Matthew 5:43-45.])

Voice: "God has failed me; he let that bad thing happen." (You blame God, thinking he did not answer your prayer, or he doesn't care about you, or he abandoned you, or he doesn't love you, or he is paying you back for a sin you committed.)

God's Truth: (It's OK to be honest and angry with God and tell him your feelings and complain to him. The following is also a good thing to say:) "Lord, I know you love me, but I don't understand why you would let this happen. I am angry at you. Help me to believe that you have a good reason and to trust that you will cause all these things to work out for good for your glory and honor. I just can't see it right now, but I continue to love and believe in you." (It will help you to talk to persons you trust about what happened and let them share your burdens and trials. Don't keep things like this to yourself. You belong to a fellowship of others who have been through similar things; you are not alone. [See Job 1:20-22; 2:7-10; 30:16-21; Romans 8:28-32.])

Voice: "God, I feel all alone. I hurt. I feel I'm in a dark time, and I can't rise above my sufferings and feelings. My heart is aching with so much pain. I feel like it will never end. I can't stop my sad feelings or my tears from flowing or control the depression that overwhelms me. Help me!"

God's Truth: "I am sorry that this world is filled with such evil, pain, and sufferings. I did not create it to be this way. The fear of death and feelings of pain and sadness that reside in you, and all people, I have overcome. You can trust me; you can trust my hope that all will one day be right. I am present with you. You will get better. All who trust me will inherit the new world I am in the process of making. Your pain is temporary. You will again have joy" (James 1:2-4; Psalm 23; 30:1-5, 10; 1 Peter 1:3-9; 2 Corinthians 1:8-10; 4:16-18; Romans 8:35-39).

Voice: "Poor me. I'm alone. Others have it better than I do. Nobody takes time for me." (Self-pity is one of the worst traps we can fall into; tears of feeling sorry for self may well up in your eyes.)

God's Truth: (As soon as possible, stop this feeling of wanting sympathy from others. Say, "No, I'm not going there, I'm not going to keep dwelling on my own situation." Think about something else or someone you can help.) God's Word says, "If there is anything worthy of praise, dwell on these things" (Philippians 4:8). God's Word also says, "Regard one another as more important than yourselves" and "look out also for the interests of others" (Philippians 2:3-4).

Here are other situations where the shield and sword are useful. If *angry or wicked people are a threat* to you, take up the shield of faith and counter with God's thoughts from scripture (Psalm 37; 140; 1 Peter 3:14). If *fear is a problem*, find a scripture you can use as an immediate and short response to help change your focus (Isaiah 41:10; Psalm 56:3-4). *Being negative or critical and grumbling and complaining* is harmful (1 Corinthians 10:5-6, 10-11). I once heard a pastor give a message about this. He said, "It affects others in negative ways, lacks proper perspective on situations, and undermines your witness of Christ living in you." The Bible says, "Do all things without grumbling or disputing" (Philippians 2:14-15). Our judgment may be true, but often we are too negative or critical and are complaining. We complain that the service in a restaurant is too slow. We complain about standing in long lines or about drivers on the road. We often judge and criticize others' faults instead of seeing the good in them. We need to change this area of our lives and grow more into the people God is creating us to be. When we catch ourselves in the act of judging, complaining, or criticizing, by using the shield of faith and the sword of the Spirit, we can say, "Stop grumbling!" Gradually the change can occur, and we start doing and being what God wants us to do and be.

SITUATIONS OF PEOPLE FIGHTING THE GOOD FIGHT

A woman who was a new believer in Christ Jesus was in a Bible study group with me. She had been involved in occult practices, and she told us that a spirit would come into her room at night and bother her. She was very frightened. The group assured her that she had the authority of Jesus to say to the spirit, "In the name of Jesus,

I command you to leave." She came back the next week and reported that it did not work. The spirit still came. She was encouraged to keep saying those words each time the spirit came. She did, and it wasn't long before the spirit left her alone, and to this day, she is still free of evil spirits and witnessing her faith in Christ (see James 4:7).

Maybe you feel there is no hope for your situation. For example, are you feeling depressed because everything seems to be going wrong; your troubles and sufferings are not going away? Are you feeling God has not answered your prayers for help and relief? Maybe your woes stem from health issues, family or work problems, or just plain having bad things happen. You have no peace, you cannot sleep, and worries and anxieties are tormenting your soul. Perhaps you are increasingly discouraged and depressed, feeling alone and sorry for yourself. Maybe you are so down you even find yourself thinking and feeling, *I would rather die than live.* Although thoughts of wanting to die are common and do not mean you are suicidal, if things do not get better, they can certainly lead to a thought-out plan for ending your life. The devil would like nothing more than to see your life ruined, and that is why we need a way to protect ourselves, to fight back, and to win. How do you stay strong in faith and be hopeful when you feel your life falling apart, and you just want to scream and have the sufferings over?

If you are at a place like this in your life, it is comforting to know that others go through similar experiences. Read the following stories of people in the Bible, and see if you can identify with any of their feelings.

- Read how a man named Job felt during his darkest days when trying to survive unbelievable sufferings. See how he honestly reveals his pain and cries out his complaints to God (Job 3:24-26; 30:16-21).

- Read Jeremiah's expressions of his down feelings in Lamentations 3:1-18.

- Read Habakkuk's description of his disturbed feelings because God was allowing bad people to wreck his world (Habakkuk 1:1-4, 13; 3:16).

- Read authors of the Psalms and see if you can identify with their experiences and feelings of suffering (Psalm 51:1-17; Psalm 88).9

- Read in Psalm 22:1-18 what is viewed by many as the thoughts of Jesus when he suffered on the cross. Jesus knows the feelings of being down and out.

In addition to these stories in the Bible, it is also helpful to share with trusted friends, fellow believers, and others to learn things they have gone through. We are not alone in our sufferings. Moreover, with God, there is a way out (1 Corinthians 10:13).

When life involves ongoing sufferings, and it seems we are losing everything, even our life, words of faith like those whose statements of suffering you just read can help us survive. Job said, "Shall we indeed accept good from God and not accept adversity?" (Job 2:10). "Though he slay me, I will hope in him" (Job 13:15). "As for me, I know that my Redeemer lives, and at the last he will take his stand on the earth. Even after my skin is destroyed, yet from my flesh I shall see God" (Job 19:25-27; compare Zechariah 14:3-9).

Other words of faith include those of Jeremiah: "This I recall to my mind, therefore I have hope." What did he recall to his mind? Read his powerful statement in Lamentations 3:21-26. When facing bad things, Habakkuk said, "I will rejoice in the God of my salvation. The Lord God is my strength" (see Habakkuk 3:17-19). The psalmist said, "Even though I walk through the valley of the shadow of death, I fear no evil, for You [God] are with me. I will dwell in the house of the Lord forever" (Psalm 23:4, 6). Knowing God the Father and believing that he will fulfill his promises, Jesus said, "If You are willing, remove this cup [death] from Me; yet not My will, but Yours be done" (Luke 22:42). At the time of his death, Jesus said, "Into Your hands I commit My spirit" (Luke 23:46; see also Acts 2:24-28).

Consider words of others, like the words of Daniel's friends when facing their imminent death: "God whom we serve is able to deliver us . . . but even if he does not, we are not going to serve

---

9. Go to https://www.americamagazine.org/faith/2017/10/20/i-am-sexual-assault-survivor-psalms-gave-me-new-words-define-myself where you will find a heart-healing description of how reading Psalm 88 helped a woman deal with years of destructive thinking and feelings due to sexual assault.

your gods" (Daniel 3:17-18). The Apostle Paul demonstrated faith and hope when, in times of despair, he could say, "We had the sentence of death within ourselves so that we would not trust in ourselves, but in God who raises the dead" (2 Corinthians 1:8-10). David, a shepherd boy, heard the discouraging words of his enemy but resisted them and, by the truths of his faith, defeated the giant (1 Samuel 17:41-47).

These people could say these things because they had a close relationship with God. God desires for us to seek him simply to experience his love and know that we can trust him (Psalm 25:1-7; Jeremiah 9:23-24). In quiet meditation, away from all distractions, it is good to draw near to God our Father and Jesus our Lord and sense the safety and peacefulness of his presence (Isaiah 30:15). Jesus invites us to come to him and find rest (Matthew 11:28; Revelation 3:20). Do you have this kind of faith in God, that he is enough and you need nothing but him? Can you claim for yourself the words of Psalm 73:25-28, "Besides you, I desire nothing on earth"? In the grip of darkness, do you believe that nothing can separate you from the love of God? That God is for you and he will freely give you all things (Romans 8:31-39)? To experience God as your close friend and to believe in the unimaginable things God has prepared for those who love him—this is a great shield of faith (1 Corinthians 2:9-12). The mind that is steadfast on God and his love, God will keep in perfect peace (Isaiah 26:3-4; John 14:27). Know God's love.

Our battles to fight the good fight most often take place in the mind (Romans 12:2). Consider the words of Iyanla Vanzant, a Christian writer, who says this: "It is hard to feel good when there is something bad going on in your life. . . . Sometimes a change of perspective may be all that it will take to transform a painful, frustrating, or shameful experience into an empowering growth experience. Whether you believe it or not, your thoughts and words determine your reality. When you change your mind, you can change your life."[10]

---

10. Iyanla Vanzant, *Faith in the Valley: Lessons for Women on the Journey to Peace* (New York: Simon & Schuster, 1996, 1998), 11, 14. A great book of meditations that helps you deal with unwanted thoughts.

TIPS FOR SPIRITUAL GROWTH

Spiritual growth is a lifetime of intentional planning and discipline. Here are eight pointers to keep in mind as you build your shield of faith and speak God's words to the enemy:

1. *Do not expect to acquire victories over dangerous thoughts and feelings in a day.* Continue to develop shields of faith to meet new challenges. The need for spiritual growth never stops so long as we are living in this world.

2. *What some call triggers are times we are more vulnerable to temptations than other times.* Vulnerable times, when wrong choices are likely to be made, can occur when we feel over-confident and proud; when we are over-tired and stressed; when we are regularly hanging out with the wrong people; or when we are in places we know will tempt us to fall. If we want to have victory, we must be aware of these times and places and try to avoid them. Something I do to overcome the temptation to look at objectionable material on my computer is to have a picture of Jesus sitting on my desk next to the computer. I am reminded that he sees what I am doing.

3. *Remember that we do not accomplish spiritual victories by ourselves.* We are co-laborers with God; it is not all on us. We trust God for his help to make the victories possible (Philippians 2:13). The Apostle Paul, writing from his own trials and sufferings, reminds believers of their need to be strengthened with power through God's Spirit in the inner self (Ephesians 3:16).

4. *God encourages us to be thankful for all things, even our problems and trials (Ephesians 5:20), not because the problems are good, but because we believe God will bring good out of them, helping us grow to be more like Jesus* (Romans 8:28-29).

5. *A shield of faith can be from other sources besides Bible passages.* Playing music or singing a favorite chorus, hymn, or spiritual song can also aid our well-being (1 Samuel 16:23; Psalm 32:7; Isaiah 12:5; Ephesians 5:19).

6. *Many negative thoughts and feelings are natural and not necessarily bad or wrong.* We have them in response or reaction to something that has happened. It is healthy to express them to God. He is a good listener, and he understands. Fortunate are we if we have friends who can do the same. However, once bad thoughts or feelings enter and take hold of us, we need to work through them and figure out what God would have us do to accomplish what is best for everyone concerned.

7. *Thinking you have to be perfect to be a good witness of your faith to others is not true.* Being honest and sharing areas of struggle and how God is helping you overcome them can be the best witness because it demonstrates the value of having God in your life.

8. *In addition to spiritual exercises like using a shield of faith and the sword of the Spirit to ward off threatening thoughts or emotions, remember that we have bodies as well as souls.* Sometimes our problems stem from bodily disorders and causes that need physical attention, like medical diagnoses, medications, or surgeries. We need to be asking God for his wisdom on what he would have us do if we suspect a bodily disorder. Body and soul are connected (Proverbs 14:30; 1 Thessalonians 5:23).

SCRIPTURES FULFILLED WHEN USING OUR SHIELD AND SWORD

When we learn to put on the shield of faith and the sword of the Spirit, which is the Word of God, we are actually practicing what many scriptures say we are to do. We are presenting our bodies a living and holy sacrifice acceptable to God (Romans 12:1). We are taking every thought captive to the obedience of Christ (2 Corinthians 10:5; Colossians 2:8). We are being firmly rooted, built up in Christ, and established in our faith (Colossians 2:6-7). We are casting all our anxieties on God because he cares for us (1 Peter 5:7). In formulating our shield of faith, we are thinking and pondering things that are true, right, honorable, lovely, and good (Philippians 4:8). We are learning to trust in the Lord rather than leaning on our own understanding (Proverbs 3:5). We are setting our minds on what the Spirit desires, not on what the flesh desires (Romans 8:5). We are crucifying the flesh with its passions and desires (Galatians 5:24). We are walking in the Spirit of God and not fulfilling the desires of the flesh (Galatians 5:16-17). We are not shrinking back to destruction, but by living our faith, we are pleasing God and preserving our souls, that we may receive the promised rewards (Hebrews 10:36-40). We are submitting to God, purifying our hearts, and resisting the devil so that he flees from us (James 4:7-8).

Not only are we doing what the Bible says to do and are blessed with the benefits God promises, we are also becoming what the Bible says we will become. Though our outer self is decaying, our inner self is being renewed day by day (2 Corinthians 4:16). In place of anxiety, the peace of God is guarding our hearts and minds in Christ Jesus (Philippians 4:6-7). God's wisdom and understanding is entering our hearts, watching over us, and delivering us from the way of evil (Proverbs 2:6-12). God, as our faithful helper, will not let our foot slip; he will keep us and protect us from all evil (Psalm 121; 2 Thessalonians 3:3). We are spiritually maturing because we are practicing having our senses trained to discern good and evil (Hebrews 5:14). We are growing confidently nearer to God to receive mercy and find grace to help us in our time of need (Hebrews 4:14-16). We are believing in God, that "greater is he who is in [us] than he who is in the world" (1 John 4:4). We are participating in the victory that overcomes the world—our faith (1 John 5:4).

Referring back to the first paragraph in this chapter, I am thinking that George Foreman did not come back and become a winner by his own self-effort. He surrounded himself with supporters and helpers. Relying on fellow believers who are wanting to grow in faith with us provides needed strength to help us succeed in our walk with Christ. We live in a tough world. We face many opposing forces that threaten to knock us down and out. To survive those forces, we need discipline, a plan, and a powerful punch. Using our faith is our most powerful punch. Let us keep learning to know God, his Word, his will, and his ways, to fight the good fight of faith.

CHAPTER 7

FAITH, WORKS, AND GOD'S PLAN TO SAVE HIS WORLD

To me, for most of my life, God has seemed like a friend. By calling him a friend, I mean that he always seems present and near, I feel drawn to him, and I am constantly engaged in talking to him as if he is a real person who hears me—which he is. I also try to listen to him. I find myself frequently asking questions, hoping to hear his answers. Questions such as, *What is life all about, and how is life to be lived?* I think most of us would like to choose and plan our own story of what life is about and how we want to live it. However, there is something wrong with that idea. The thing that's wrong is we cannot make that choice and have our lives turn out to be the best they can be. In a world like ours, where evil exists, life always gets either somewhat or greatly messed up, and we meet disappointment. Even for the most successful of us, death cuts off what we love. The truth is, God already has a plan in which he has the best life for us in mind. His plan is best, for he knows the desires of our hearts, and his story takes into account our freedom of choice. His plans for us include a grand and most satisfying life, and if given the choice, we would choose the life he plans. Once we agree to trust our lives to God and let his story unfold, we will realize it is what we would have chosen if we had only known. The greatest possible joy and fulfillment of who we are and what we desire comes when we enter God's plans and realize our place within them. To sum up what I just said, I simply mean to point out two things: that we have freedom of choice, and at the same time, God has already determined what is best, knowing who we are collectively and as individuals.

I've said in earlier writings that I believe God has created us with freedom of choice, within certain boundaries, of course, and moreover that God determines things as he ordains them to be. The Bible verifies a mystifying principle I once learned from a college science professor's observation of nature, in which he concluded, "The truth lies simultaneous at both ends." For example, we notice in the Bible that Jesus is both God and man, and that God is sovereign and humans have free will. God does not force us to choose to be in his story; he simply offers it to us. It may be true that much of the personal life we are now living may be accurate and satisfying in terms of who we are, but it takes God to fill it out and complete it. We, and our world, have become unlike the way God created them to be. This world God made for us has been corrupted, and even though a remnant of God's goodness remains, human nature, and all that is in the world, needs to be freed from its destructive imperfections and death (Romans 7:24; 8:20-23; Hebrews 2:14-15). We may not understand why God allows evils to continue and why we must endure pain and suffering, but we do know God has given us his plan for saving the world (John 3:17; 1 John 4:14).

In this chapter, we shall not only consider God's plan to save his world and us, but also the often-misunderstood role of faith and works in that plan. The Bible is clear that God chooses to accomplish much of his will through people. Thus, God became human like us (Philippians 2:5-9), and his salvation plan is accomplished foremost through the man Christ Jesus (1 Timothy 2:3-5). The words *in Christ*, or *in him*, occur over one hundred and sixty times in the Apostle Paul's New Testament writings. These words appear at least ten times in Ephesians 1:1-14, where God describes his plan in considerable detail. God's plan for saving his world, and us who live in the world, is what the Bible as a whole is all about. That is why it is such an important book to understand. The Bible tells us we can regain the goodness of our original humanity by having the likeness of God restored in us—that is, by becoming like the one who is truly the embodiment of what it means to be human, Jesus, the Christ (Romans 5:17; 1 John 3:2; Romans 8:29). Through our faith in God's Son, we have victory over a corrupt world and its limitations (1 John 5:4-5). God is restoring his created world through Christ Jesus and his Holy Spirit and with the cooperating work of his not-yet-perfected people (Luke 10:1-9; Ephesians 2:10).

THE ROLE OF FAITH IN SALVATION

No one is more fitting to teach us about the role of faith and works in God's salvation than a man named Abraham. We shall begin by looking at five passages in the Bible to understand what Abraham teaches us about faith and works. The five passages are Genesis 12:1-3, Genesis 15:1-6, Galatians 3:6-14, Romans 4, and Hebrews 11:8-19. Romans 4 shall be our primary source, with support from these other portions of scripture.

Abraham is the chosen teacher because he is a recognized source on the subject of faith and works. He is called the father of our faith, the father of all believers in Christ Jesus (Romans 4:16; Galatians 3:7). Abraham does not primarily teach faith by explaining faith to us; he shows us faith through the story of his life. He shows us what faith in God looks like as it develops and grows through the trials, testings, and questionings of life's experiences. His faith blossoms into an unflinching belief in God and his Word and a trusting obedience to God's will. Therefore, "What shall we say that Abraham, our forefather according to the flesh, has found?" (Romans 4:1).

Abraham found that God's promised salvation was not based on any work of his own, not based on keeping God's laws, and not based on being good enough to earn it; God's salvation was given to him simply because he believed God and his promises (Romans 4:1-5). To see how faith was involved in Abraham's salvation, we go back to the story of God's promises to him in Genesis 12:1-3, 13:15, and 15:1-6. God promised to provide for him a land as an eternal dwelling place, not for him only but for all peoples of the world, including those in our present day and beyond. We see this in Genesis 12:3 where God promised Abraham, "In you all the families of the earth will be blessed." In Genesis 15:4 God promised, "One will come forth from your own body." What God meant by this is that the one who would be the savior of the world would come through Abraham's lineage (Galatians 3:16; Matthew 1:1). According to Jesus, Abraham knew about Christ's coming day (John 8:56).

To inherit God's salvation promises, Abraham, as a sinful person, needed to be made righteous before a holy God; he needed to be justified by God. As we see in the Genesis passages, God justified Abraham based on his faith. When Abraham believed God's promise to make him a father of many nations, to bless all nations through him, and to bless him with a son, he was reckoned by God to be righteous (Genesis 15:6; Romans 4:3). The point is made clear in Romans that if one works for something, he receives the wages due him or her. But to one who believes in God who justifies the ungodly, that person's faith is credited as righteousness (Romans 4:4-5). What Abraham received when God declared him to be righteous by faith was the blessing of forgiveness for all his sins (Romans 4:6-8; Psalms 32:1-2). Along with this blessing, he was guaranteed to inherit the world (Romans 4:13). Someone defined the word *justified* as "just as if I'd never sinned." *Justified* means, in a legal courtroom sense, the judge has declared you "not guilty." This makes us at peace with God (Romans 5:1).

Again, how was righteousness credited to Abraham (Romans 4:10-12)? Was righteousness credited because he was circumcised? No; circumcision came later as a seal of his righteousness by faith. Was righteousness credited because he obeyed God's laws? No; God's laws, given through Moses, came later. This act of justification by God was before circumcision and without law keeping so that Abraham would be the father of all who believe. Righteousness is a gift of God's grace for all people. The statement in Genesis that Abraham would be the father of many nations meant that all people are invited to receive God's salvation, by faith, apart from circumcision and law keeping.

Regarding a promised son, Abraham struggled in his faith. Abraham and his wife were old and past the age of having children (Genesis 17:17-19). At first, Abraham tried to fulfill God's promise on his own by having a child through his wife's maidservant. This was not God's intention. Abraham had to grow to believe that God could, and would, give them the promised son by a miracle. He must believe that God was capable of "giving life to the dead and calling into being that which does not exist" (Romans 4:17-21). When Abraham saw how God was able to do the impossible, allowing his aged wife to give birth to a son, it strengthened his faith. Instead of being weak in faith, he became stronger in faith. We have the same faith when we believe God's promise to raise us from the dead, not only physically (1 Corinthians 6:14) but spiritually as well (John 3:3; 5:24-25). For us to inherit God's promises and experience salvation, resurrection from death to life is a miracle God asks us to believe and receive (John 1:12-13; 1 Peter 1:3-4).

An even greater test of Abraham's faith came later when God asked him to sacrifice his promised son on an altar (Genesis 22). *Wait a minute; why? This doesn't make sense!* Imagine how difficult it would be for him to destroy his beloved son whom God promised as part of his salvation plan. Yet by this time in his experiences with God, Abraham trusted God so completely that he reasoned God would do one of two things: either provide a sacrifice to take the place of his son (Genesis 22:7-8), or, if his son died, God would raise him from the dead, thus preserving the promise (Hebrews 11:17-19). Abraham obeyed God based on his faith in God's proven power to do the impossible, and because Abraham believed and obeyed, God reconfirmed his promise that "in your seed all the nations of the earth shall be blessed" (Genesis 22:18). This event involving Abraham and his son gives us a picture, or foreshadowing, of the meaning of God's promised Son, the Messiah to come.

Think about it: is our faith like Abraham's faith? His strong faith did not happen overnight, any more than ours does. His faith was made strong over many years through many testings, as is ours. When you study the life of Abraham, you will see Abraham as an imperfect person, yet he was called out to fulfill a special role in God's salvation story. Abraham exercised faith in what God told him to do, but notice that he did not receive in his lifetime all God promised him. His faith needed to take the future into account and welcome the fact that God would be faithful to bring him, along with all other believers, to the promised eternal land and city, a far better country than this world offers (Hebrews 11:13-16).

Salvation comes by faith in what God says and promises. What God did through his promised Son's death on a cross, and through understanding and placing our faith in what that means through the cross and our faith, God grants forgiveness and declares us to be righteous. Placing faith in God's Christ, and acknowledging him as Lord, is what allows God to save us and his world (John 1:1-3, 10-13; 1 John 5:11-13). Faith believes that by sticking with Jesus and trusting him, we too will take part, with Abraham, in God's planned restoration of all things and in his promised destination (Psalm 23; 2 Corinthians 1:9-10).

CONFUSION OVER FAITH AND WORKS IN GOD'S SALVATION STORY

One area of confusion is over how one gets to heaven. Most religious people, including some who call themselves Christians, think their good works will earn their salvation and eternal life in heaven. Their belief goes something like this: *If I am good, and my good outweighs my bad, then I'm certain to be acceptable to God.* Or, *If I obey what God wants me to do, I'm in.* The Bible is clear that being declared right with God is a prerequisite to heaven and is based on faith and not our works (John 1:12-13; 3:16; Acts 10:43; 11:13-18; 16:29-31; Romans 3:21-26; Ephesians 2:8-9; Galatians 2:16). As stated above, it is clear that we are justified, declared not guilty, by faith.

Another area of confusion is the meaning of heaven. Unfortunately, many people's view of God's salvation is limited to their belief that they will go to heaven when they die. But faith in salvation involves much more than the hope of one day going to heaven. For one thing, it involves participating in God's present plan to save his world. One way we do this is by demonstrating to the people around us what heaven will be like.

Something else that seems confusing when it comes to our salvation is whether faith alone saves us or whether our works must be involved. James, in his writing of God's Word, says something that would seem to say the opposite of what Paul says in Romans. James says, "You see that a man is justified by works and not by faith alone" (James 2:24). James refers to Abraham and says Abraham was justified by works when he offered up Isaac on the altar (James 2:21). Does this contradict the truth that we are justified (declared not guilty) by faith (Romans 3:28; 4:2)? No. James is only making the point that faith, the kind that saves us, will prove itself by the life we live—that is, by the works we do in loving, voluntary service to God. If we have faith that saves us, it will be evident by our works.

Paul addresses the same issue as James, but in a different manner. We cannot have faith and then think we can willingly continue to sin, believing God will forgive us (see Romans 6:1-2). The differing statements by Paul and James can be resolved as follows. If anyone thinks he or she can be saved by good works, they need to hear that salvation is by faith and not by works (Romans 3:28). If anyone thinks that we are saved by faith and it doesn't matter how we live morally, they need to hear that faith without works is dead (James 2:17, 26).

THE ROLE OF WORKS IN SALVATION

Works are a result of experiencing God's love, forgiveness, and new life in Christ Jesus. We do them because God has chosen us to be co-laborers in accomplishing his plans for restoring the world (1 Corinthians 3:9; Colossians 4:11; Ephesians 2:10; 1 Thessalonians 1:2-10). God's salvation plan was helped along toward completion when Abraham obeyed what God told him to do. Doing what God says to do is to co-operate with the Lord in helping to show the world what God's kingdom is like and to invite others to join (Luke 10:2-9). Salvation does not mean we simply believe in Jesus so we can one day go to heaven. Salvation involves us in our Lord's work. As Christians, we will better accept our role in God's redeeming work if we understand two things: (1) who we are as God's people and (2) our motivation for joining him in his work.

First, who are we? We are believers in Christ Jesus who have been born into his kingdom (John 3:3). God says, "He rescued us from the domain of darkness, and transferred us to the kingdom of his beloved Son, in whom we have redemption, the forgiveness of sins" (Colossians 1:13-14). This means we no longer see ourselves primarily as citizens of this earthly world but as citizens of the kingdom of God (Philippians 3:20; Ephesians 2:19-22). We are people belonging to another world who are passing through this corrupted world on the way to God's glorious future (Hebrews 11:8-10, 13-16; 1 Peter 2:9-12). We have been transferred from this world's systems of operation to the Lord's systems. Just as we obey human laws and relate to people according to the world's ways, now we obey God's laws and relate to people according to God's ways (Exodus 19:5-6; 1 Peter 2:9-17). We are still in the world, but we are not of the world (John 17:14-16, 20-21). We are citizens of God's kingdom, yielding to Christ as our king and learning to live by his instructions and benevolent ways. We are part of a social structure, his church, organized by him for the purpose of continuing the good works of our Lord Jesus (Matthew 16:18; John 14:11-14). This earth, which God will also redeem, is a part of God's coming kingdom (Romans 8:19-21). Therefore, because it will continue to be our home in the future, we still have a responsibility to care for God's earth.

Second, why do we involve ourselves in his work? Living for God is who we are because God has given us a new heart. As part of being converted from this world into God's kingdom, Jesus baptized us with the Holy Spirit (Luke 3:15-16; Acts 1:4-5). Christian theologies have differing beliefs about when the Holy Spirit enters the believer's life. Whether the Holy Spirit enters into us from the time we put faith in Christ to save us, or during our water baptism, or as a later blessing, the important thing to know is that, as a result of our faith in Christ Jesus, God has given the Holy Spirit to dwell in us (James 4:5; 1 Corinthians 6:19). Through his indwelling Spirit, God has given us a heart that desires what God desires (Ezekiel 36:24-27). The experience of his love has been put into our hearts through the Holy Spirit who was given to us (Romans 5:5). Because of God's lovingkindness and mercy, we want to give our bodies to serve his cause and join in his work (Romans 12:1-2). We serve God because he has loved us, and experiencing his love causes us to love as he loves (1 John 4:19, 2:5-6). As we enter deeper into that relationship of love with our heavenly Father and his Son, Jesus, we are increasingly being motivated to hear his Word and do his will (John 14:18-26; Luke 8:21). The key to motivation is to grow in love with God.

SEEING THE BIG PICTURE

Even though we accept our role as co-laborers with God, Christians can feel lost and unsure of what God wants us to do. It helps us to know what to do if we can see the big picture of what God is doing and where he is taking us. The importance of seeing the big picture is well illustrated in the movie version of Tolkien's story of *The Hobbit*. The lead character, Bilbo, and his companions are lost in a forest. They knew where they were to be going, but in the forest, they became confused, disoriented, frustrated, and depressed. They encountered various problems, and their preoccupation with those problems was a factor in losing their way. Bilbo climbs a tree to get above the darkness, looks around, and sees the truth about where they are. He recognizes in the distance the place they are trying to get to and sees which way to go. He climbs down and helps the others know the way. Although he and his companions must still travel through the forest, encountering many dangers, because of seeing the big picture from a higher viewpoint, he and his companions are no longer confused and lost.

How can we see God's big picture? When we read the Bible from beginning to end, we get the big picture of God's plan. Let's refresh our memory of the big picture presented in chapter two of this book. God created a good world, but it became ruined when evil entered and all fell into death. God's plan is to redeem and rescue the world from evil and death by sending Christ Jesus into the world to make it possible. Through chosen messengers, God is calling out a people to know him and is changing them into a new creation in Christ (Romans 8:29; 2 Corinthians 5:17). He is forming his people into a loving fellowship that is equipping them to become mature in Jesus so they can participate in his salvation works (Ephesians 4:11-16).

As the main character in God's story, Jesus shows us the big picture through the life he lived among us. When Jesus came to earth long ago, his life, works, and teachings gave us a preview of what his coming kingdom, as revealed in the book of Revelation, would be like. He healed diseases and physical deformities, raised people from the dead, fed the hungry, gave hope to the poor, and demonstrated power to eliminate nature's life-threatening disastrous storms. He quieted people's inner storms, forgiving their guilt and giving them his peace. In his presence, evil forces fled, wrongs done to fellow humans were not allowed, and false religious worship of God was corrected. Jesus was kind to people and offered the hope of a coming kingdom of righteousness, peace, and joy (Romans 14:17). It will be a perfect and love-filled world without any evil. How strange that the kind of life we humans say we long for and want, the kind of life demonstrated by Jesus, was met with cruelty, scorn, and crucifixion. But his death on a cross was the one and only way possible for God to show how much he loved us and to enable the saving of his created world (Acts 4:12; 1 Timothy 2:5-6; Romans 5:8-11).

When Jesus came to life again and departed from this world, he left his disciples with the task of carrying on his works of salvation (Matthew 28:16-20; John 14:12-14). Through the gift of his Holy Spirit, he gave them his power to do his work until he returns (Acts 1:4-8). Those works are like the ones Jesus did as described in the previous paragraph. The disciples were to pass on his life of faith, hope, and love to all people. When biblical faith, hope, and love are truly understood, experienced, and practiced by believers, there is nothing equivalent to it in this world. What a privilege to share such a life with others. God is at work, saving his created world and its people through Christ Jesus, and we have a part in it when we exhibit Christ's faith, hope, and works of love to those around us. That is our work, and knowing God's overall goal keeps us moving in the right direction. That is the value of seeing the big picture.

What Our Role in Christ's Work Looks Like

God calls most of us to live a normal, everyday life. A normal life means growing to be like Jesus, raising our families, enjoying the world God made for us, meeting the needs of people where we work and live, and shining as lights in a dark world by living as God wants, thus exhibiting God's ways to people around us (1 Peter 2:9-12).

Being part of a church helps us find volunteer things we can do that promote God's kingdom work. God needs people to do his work through their everyday lives in their communities, always growing spiritually and getting better at it. We are to be like the man Jesus healed, whom he told to "go home to your people and report to them what great things the Lord has done for you, and how he had mercy on you" (Mark 5:19-20). We are reporting what God does for us by what we say, by the example we set for how we live, and by the good works that we do.

God calls some to fulfill specific assignments like taking leadership positions in the church, becoming missionaries at home or to other parts of the world, or engaging in other special tasks Jesus wants them to do. I have a missionary friend in Africa whose work is to train teachers so they can teach children the ways of God. Her special instruction from God comes from Micah 4:2, which says, "Come and let us go up to the mountain of the Lord and to the house of the God of Jacob, that he may teach us about his ways and that we may walk in his paths." She sees what God wants to do, and she helps do it. She is training teachers who will teach others about Christ and how to walk in his ways, thus bringing God's salvation to that part of the world (2 Timothy 2:2). God calls all of us to support God's workers, helping them be able to fulfill their tasks (3 John 5-8).

I have witnessed many of God's good works being done through his people. I have seen unloved people loved, messed-up people get their lives together, marriages reunited, lonely people find a caring family, compassionate people meet other people's needs, and fearful people find peace. Christ's people have done, and continue to do, more good for the world than the world will ever know. That work includes building schools to educate the illiterate, orphanages to care for the homeless, and elder care facilities; feeding the poor, giving relief following catastrophes, and teaching health care; providing medical services, agricultural projects, and loans to help the poor start self-sustaining businesses; fighting for human rights like the abolition of slavery, rescuing girls caught in sex trafficking, faithfully proclaiming the good news of life-changing forgiveness in Christ, and on and on. Every part we do, no matter how small, is important. Jesus said, even a cup of cold water given to meet a need will receive its reward (Matthew 10:42). When God's kingdom, in all its fullness, comes on earth, we will have had a part in making it happen—though we may not always know it.

The kingdom of God is where Jesus reigns as King over his people. When you became a born-again follower of Jesus, you became a child of the King and a citizen in his kingdom (Matthew 13:24-30, 36-43; Colossians 1:13-14). You are now under the reign of the King and so are subject to living the lifestyle of his people by living under his loving rule. You are part of the people of God on earth. We are showcases for outsiders to see what living can be like in God's kingdom of heaven (1 Peter 2:9-10). This is what God wants unbelieving people to see. We are lights in the darkness (Ephesians 5:8-10; Matthew 5:14-16). We are lifelines for people who are drowning. We are witnesses to the grace of God so others can see the difference Jesus can make in the lives of people who love and follow him. We are continually changing to reflect the life of heaven to the people around us. How we live in this age of the world is a prelude to enjoying the next.

CARING FOR THE EARTH IS PART OF OUR WORK

The earth is the Lord's, and the earth will be redeemed along with many of its people (Psalm 24:1; Isaiah 65:17-18, 25; 66:1-2; Romans 8:18-23). The earth is our home, and both now and in the future, it is a part of God's kingdom. It is clear that we are to enjoy our work and the world God gave us, for he said to the first humans, "You may eat of everything, except of whatever brings evil into your life" (Genesis 1:28-29; 2:15-17). When God says, "Do not love the world nor the things in the world," does he mean we cannot enjoy the pleasures and exciting discoveries of this world (1 John 2:15)? Not at all! "Do not love the world" means don't be involved in its lustful evils; don't make the things of the world your God. Because God created the earth to be our home (Psalm 115:16), he means for us to discover its secrets and enjoy all the good things it offers that benefit our lives.

God, in his kindness, has given us all things richly to enjoy (1 Timothy 6:17; Acts 14:16-17). God "causes his sun to rise on the evil and the good, and sends rain on the righteous and the unrighteous"

(Matthew 5:45). All earthly gifts are evidence of God's kindness. Even unbelievers benefit from discoveries on earth by enjoying things like improved health care, communications, and travel. Unlike many people of the world, we are to acknowledge that all is from God and give thanks for the pleasures and benefits we receive. Surprisingly, the Bible says the kindness of God can lead people to repentance and new life (Romans 2:4). When people express how blessed they are by their good fortunes in life, we would do well to mention to them, "Isn't God good and kind to give you and me all these things that make our lives enjoyable?" We can also remind them that God, in his kindness sent us a savior (Titus 3:4-5).

Again, I emphasize that God gave us the task of ruling over and caring for the earth (Genesis 1:28; 2:15). We respect God's present creation, and we take good care of it, for that is what he told us to do in this age, and that is what we will do in the next age. Some will say, "Why take care of this world? It is corrupted with evil and is passing away, and God promised to give us a new one in the future." My reply is, "Do we say the same about our bodies? They are also corrupted with evil, they are passing away, and God promises us a new body when Jesus comes again. Do we neglect the care of our bodies because someday we will have a new one?" God's mandate is to care for both our bodies and the earth. We care about them and take care of them because they are of great worth to God, he uses them as instruments to meet needs and minister his love, and his purpose is to restore them to their former glory. That is what we are working toward by caring for people and the earth.

DANGERS ARE EXPECTED IN DOING GOD'S WORK

Unfortunately, because we live in a world of evil, we must endure hard times and sufferings to get where we are going. We must accept these times and allow God to strengthen and mold us through them (James 1:2-4; Romans 5:3-5). Through trials, we are continually learning to overcome our fears and character defects and are becoming more like Jesus (1 Peter 1:3-9; 2:20-23; 3:13-16; 4:1-5, 12-19; 5:6-11). We may face temptations and battles along the way (2 Thessalonians 1:3-5) and even suffer some defeats. But in the end, we triumph (1 Corinthians 15:57; 2 Corinthians 2:14). Aim to experience a grand entrance into the coming kingdom of our Lord Jesus, with joy that we have fulfilled what God has called us to be and do, and with confidence that, in Christ, we are forever victorious over evil and death. We are to be co-rulers with Christ (2 Timothy 2:11-12; Revelation 20:4), inheriting all things that belong to him (Ephesians 1:13-14; Romans 8:16-17) and marveling at the grandeur of all that God has prepared and planned for our never-ending and never-boring existence in the Father's new heaven and new earth (1 Corinthians 2:9; 2 Peter 3:11-13; Revelation 21:3-7).

Many things that happen to us are not good, but God can bring good out of them. What he says is true: "God causes all things to work together for good to those who love God, to those who are called according to his purpose" (Romans 8:28). Satan works to destroy what God wants to do in and through us (John 8:44; 10:10). To defeat the enemy, we must take up the armor God gives us and fight the good fight of faith (Ephesians 6:10-20). Though filled with dangers and ups and downs, we dare to be part of God's adventure because we believe God exists and rewards those who seek him (Hebrews 11:6).

God encourages us with words from the Apostle Paul. He wrote, "So then, my beloved, just as you have always obeyed, not as in my presence only, but now much more in my absence, work out your salvation with fear and trembling; for it is God who is at work in you, both to will and to work for his good pleasure" (Philippians 2:12-13). As co-laborers with God in the work of his kingdom, try this exercise, as an individual and as a church body:

What work for the Lord's kingdom have you done? Make a list of as many things as possible that fit this category. You may be pleasantly surprised and encouraged to see how you are involved in the work of the Lord. As we grow spiritually, our influence will increase, and God will be glorified through us.

Those who realize that God wants us to become part of his solution for a new world can begin by praying something like the following:

Lord, you are holy and righteous, untouched by evil. We are unholy and unrighteous, filled with self-centeredness and a pride that makes us think we know better than you do. Many of our attributes and behaviors are far from who you created us to be. Thank you that through the cross of your Son, Jesus, reconciliation with you and others becomes possible. It is through your grace and power that restoration of all things becomes a reality. Learning to know your will and ways and how to live by faith is the path we want to take back to you. We have come to believe that we are perfectly loved by you (1 John 3:1; 4:16) and that you want only good for us (Romans 8:28-32). We understand that in this world, we may suffer bodily and emotionally, but we know you have a plan to use those sufferings for your wise and good purposes. Help us to seek and desire you as our greatest treasure and to seek your kingdom of righteousness, love, peace, and joy as our greatest goal and destination. We are your beloved creation. Save us. Amen.

CHAPTER 8

FAITH, GOD'S EARTH, AND SCIENCE

Most people may not care about this subject, but I include a chapter about faith and science because there is a prevailing belief among many that faith and science do not mix and are to be kept separate. Western civilization is largely influenced by science, and when science presents findings that disagree with the Bible, this becomes a huge stumbling block for those who want to have faith in what the Bible says. Needless to say, believers in the Bible also create problems with the scientific community when they argue that the Bible is right and scientific findings are wrong. The common person who becomes acquainted with the controversial issues may take one side over the other, try to reconcile the two, or simply not care. Because of ignorance, misunderstandings, or confusion, I hope to at least help clarify some of the issues and bring science and faith closer together.

When technical, scientific, philosophical, and theological language is used to discuss this subject, most people, including myself, do not understand what is being talked about. If someone is using big words to tell me something, I might say, "Hey, wait. I don't get it. Could you bring that *down to earth* for me?" We use the expression "down to earth" when we want to make a difficult subject easier to understand. Somehow we must bring the issues of faith and science down to earth in order to get a better grasp of them. Maybe that is why God the Father sent Jesus the Son *down to earth*—to give us a better grasp of who God is and what he is like.

When approaching the subject of faith and science, many in our modern culture are aware of the conflicts between the two. For example, Exodus events, found in the biblical book of Exodus, are the historical events that supposedly happened when the Israelites were freed from their slavery and exited out of Egypt. In the scientific studies of archaeology, there is disagreement over whether or not there is evidence that the Exodus events of the Bible really happened. A more familiar example of controversy between faith and science is the disagreement involving Creation versus evolution. The purpose of this chapter is not to try to settle arguments involving the Bible and science but to point out and help clarify some of the issues. If I argue for anything, it is that faith and science belong together.

WHAT THE BIBLE SAYS ABOUT THE NATURAL WORLD AND GOD'S EARTH

The approach I want to take in this chapter is to begin by stating four things the Bible says about the physical world, its earth, and God. I will then attempt to explain what each statement means in its biblical context and, in so doing, comment on some of the controversial issues involving faith and science.

1. God created the heavens and the earth (Genesis 1:1).

2. God created humans to rule over all the earth and subdue it (Genesis 1:26, 28).

3. The earth has been corrupted and cursed, but God will one day restore it to its intended purposes (Genesis 3:17-18; Isaiah 24:1, 5-6; Romans 8:19-23).

4. What we observe in the physical world reveals something about the God who created it (Romans 1:20).

(1) GOD CREATED THE HEAVENS AND THE EARTH

God's written salvation story begins this way: "In the beginning, God created the *heavens and the earth*" (Genesis 1:1, emphasis added). This phrase means that God caused the earth, its atmosphere, and the entire universe to come into being. Christians believe God exists prior to, and separate from, the visible universe, and therefore nature is not God. Furthermore, "The earth is the Lord's, and all it contains, the world, and those who dwell in it" (Psalm 24:1). All belongs to God.

"In the beginning was the *Word*, and the *Word* was with God, and the *Word* was God. He was in the beginning with God. All things came into being through him, and apart from him nothing came into being that has come into being" (John 1:1-3, emphasis added). This *Word*, Christ Jesus, came as a human and lived among us (John 1:14). Jesus existed as part of the Trinitarian God and was the instrument through whom God spoke and the worlds came into existence. When Jesus became human like us, we caught a glimpse of *Jesus as the Word* when he spoke and things happened. For example, when he spoke to nature and a storm ceased (Matthew 8:23-27), or when he spoke to the dead and they came back to life (Luke 7:11-16; John 11:32-44), or when he healed people with a word (Matthew 8:5-13).

"*By faith* we understand that the *worlds* were *prepared by the word of God*, so that what is seen was not made out of things which are visible" (Hebrews 11:3, emphasis added). The word *worlds* is commonly interpreted as God's material universe and his appointed ages in time. The word *prepared* implies that God put together the earth and world with a purpose in mind, one purpose being to make a home for the care of humans, providing for their needs and enjoyments. The phrase "by the word of God" refers to the often repeated, "God said" in Genesis 1 (see also Psalm 33:6). The word *faith* is used because humans were not there to witness how the world and life began, so the cause of the world's origin is known by faith in God's written Word. Although God is unseen, evidence of his existence is seen through observations of what he made and through discoveries of ancient and modern science.

Faith, as discussed in this book, is essential because we are limited in knowledge, nothing is proven 100 percent certain, and faith bridges the gap between uncertainty and certainty. It allows us to live happily with what makes sense to us and with what gives us security at any given point in time. Without faith, all is up for grabs and life is in turmoil and chaos. We must exercise faith in the accuracy of our senses and that facts presented to us can be trusted. Although we may differ in what we see or think to be true, without faith, we would be without a compass to ground us and guide our lives. Faith is necessary for both a believer in God and a believer in no God. Even one who does not believe in the existence of God must exercise faith that he does not exist. The truth is, no matter what evidence one uses for or against God, without 100 percent proof, one must choose by faith to accept the reality of God—or not.

Unfortunately, in our present world, we as humans, for various reasons, like to find ways to separate God from this world and from our lives. It would seem that we want to be our own gods and not have to yield to the God who created everything. For some, science offers a way to make faith in God seem either unnecessary or foolish. Because of misunderstandings between science and faith, many find in science a reason to do away with God, or at least to separate him from our world and daily living. Following are three reasons commonly used to create separation between faith and science or between God and the physical world.

First, when speaking of faith and science, a statement we hear in modern culture is that faith deals with religion and mystical things, while science deals with reason and physical things. By equating faith with religious things and equating science with reason and physical things, we create in our thinking two different worlds that are unrelated and opposed to each other. Implied is that faith needs no reason because it deals only with beliefs, and science needs no faith because it deals only with facts. It seems this idea of faith and science as separate worlds is based on partial truth rather than the whole truth and is thus the result of misunderstanding.

A second reason used to create separation between faith and science is to say that humans invented the idea of God. There is a belief that before science, humans were primitive and uneducated and needed a god to explain the world. A belief by many moderns is that humans no longer need God to explain the world because science is able to explain the world. The Bible would agree that humans have invented their own gods, but that is not true in every case. Some did not invent God, but God, in various ways, made himself known to them (Hebrews 1:1-2). One way he makes himself known is by making the world so we would be able to see him in his creation. "That which is known about God is evident within them; for God made it evident to them . . . through what has been made" (see Romans 1:19-23). People create their own gods when they reject the true God.

A third way some try to separate God from the physical world is to eliminate all things having to do with God from scientific endeavors. Here are three examples.

1. Some scientists present from their scientific viewpoint that the world is entirely of natural origin; God was not involved. Some would even say that the material world is the only reality that exists. Therefore, science can discover and provide what is good for humanity without a need for God. For example, it is becoming a popular belief that science can reverse aging and create long life, possibly even eternal life. Modern-day people are led to believe that science can do what has been thought to be only what God can do. Biblical Christians would differ and say that God is the only eternal being who is without beginning or end and that he is needed as the giver and sustainer of life. As our Creator, he cares about us and remains involved in our well-being. It would make sense to teach the sciences along with a Creator God because they inform each other and belong together. As the Bible says, "All things have been created through him and for him . . . and *in him all things hold together*" (Colossians 1:16-17, emphasis added). God remains involved and needed in this world.

2. Because science determined that the physical is the only reality, there have followed certain beliefs. One is that the human body is entirely physical and does not have a spirit. The brain can explain all of life's experiences, even apparent spiritual experiences, thus eliminating God. Of course, the Bible disagrees with this view of human nature

by saying that humans are made with body and spirit. The Bible says that death results when the spirit is separated from the body (James 2:26). Jesus raised a dead girl who lived again when her spirit returned (Luke 8:52-55).

3. Some define *science* as the study of the natural world using only observations and methods involving the natural world. God is thus excluded from a study of the natural world. This definition was carried over into our public education system when we made a law that religion does not belong in science and must not be taught in our science classrooms. Unfortunately, this law has resulted in greater rifts between faith and science and consequently removed from schools the study of how God fits into, and benefits, our study of the natural world.

There is a book titled *God's Two Books*, written by Kenneth J. Howell.[11] Christians believe God has written two books. One is the Bible and the other is nature. These two books give us answers to questions about God and the world we observe. Since God is the author of both, Christians expect that what is revealed in nature and what is revealed in his written Word, when rightly observed, will be in total agreement. Any apparent disagreements must be due to some error or misunderstanding on either side, or on both sides, for the God revealed in his written Word would not say one thing in the Bible and a contradictory thing in nature. If all the facts were in, and the world and the Bible were accurately observed and interpreted, they would both agree. The problem is that the facts are not yet all in, so it may seem they do not agree. However, the more discoveries science makes and the more accurately the Bible is interpreted, the more they are shown to agree. We must decide what we can reasonably believe based on the current evidence— what things in the Bible are clear or unclear, what things in science are clear or unclear, and what things are to be held open until further information becomes available.

---

11. Kenneth J. Howell, *God's Two Books: Copernican Cosmology and Biblical Interpretation in Early Modern Science* (Notre Dame, Indiana: Univ. of Notre Dame Press, 2002).

(2) Ruling and Subduing the Earth

Another statement the Bible says about God's earth is that God created humans to rule over the earth and subdue it (Genesis 1:26, 28). We are under his authority and responsible to him to take care of the atmosphere, land, water, plants, and animals. To have this responsibility means at least two things.

First, as Creator, God owns all (Psalm 24:1; 50:11-12; 89:11). He made the earth to support life, and he made it to be the home of humans. He has turned the earth over to them to be the earth's stewards (Genesis 2:15). As stewards, God has entrusted us with the care of the earth. Because he created us in his image, we share his goodness, and he expects that we will not abuse and misuse the earth and its contents for greedy gain or destructive pleasures. We are to take care of the earth, enjoying it, preserving its beauty, and using it as a way to meet the needs of self and others.

Second, subduing the earth means, in part, discovering the hidden resources that God has built into his creation and harnessing them for beneficial purposes. As we read the story of the Bible, it was not long after Creation that humans made clothes for themselves, cultivated their land to produce food, discovered metals, learned to make musical instruments and tools, and used earth's resources to invent and build things that benefited their lives (Genesis 4:2, 17, 21-22). Ruling and subduing the earth surely includes doing satisfying work, discovering earth's many hidden secrets, and using them to benefit all people. Such is our intended, God-given role: to enjoy fulfilling work and bring creation under our control.

Science involves observing and discovering how the world works. Scientists are people who make a living at doing science. When scientists observe physical things in the world and report about their discoveries, we learn many things we did not know. Applied science happens when people take the newly discovered information and use those discoveries to do things or invent things that will make our lives better. Scientific discoveries help improve many areas of life, including agriculture, physical health, communication systems, travel, weather predictions, psychological and sociological workings of people, household appliances, personal care items, and so forth.

We don't have to be scientists to observe the world and discover things. Each of us, as we go through life, finds ways to make life more productive and rewarding. We use and appreciate what God has given us to enhance our lives.

Unfortunately, with the introduction of evil into our world, subduing the earth has become much more difficult. We discover the importance of living the moral principles God has put into us, because wrongdoing corrupts and cripples our efforts to enjoy life, and we learn to be responsible stewards in adequately caring for the world. When we live as God created us to live, we bring the life of God into our earthly experiences, and we understand that we now have a responsibility to subdue evil. How do we subdue evil? We overcome evil by doing good (Romans 12:21), thus helping the world see how God means for life to be lived. When we overcome evil by doing good, we are bringing to earth a bit of what God's kingdom is like. We are taking back a piece of God's world and helping it to be what God wants it to be, and will one day make it to be, when he comes.

(3) THE EARTH, CURSED AND RESTORED

God's written story reveals that nature has been cursed but that God will one day restore it to its intended purposes (Genesis 3:17-18; Isaiah 65:17, 25; 66:22; Romans 8:19-23). This hope is for all who care to believe it. Jesus taught his people to pray, "Thy kingdom come on earth as it is in heaven." When Jesus lived on earth, he demonstrated the power of God's kingdom in heaven when he showed what the kingdom of God on earth would look like under his reign as king. By Jesus's ruling and subduing the earth, he was able to heal diseases, raise the dead to life, eliminate nature's storms, erase guilt through forgiveness, and create a new and righteous people to inhabit his new and righteous world (Revelation 21:3-5; 2 Corinthians 5:17; 2 Peter 3:13). Without God, many lose their sense of moral guidance and let evil take over their lives. That is why people are subject to abusing our planet and each other. Because of evil, the Bible says the earth is wearing out and will eventually die (Isaiah 51:6; Matthew 24:35; Hebrews 1:10-11).

However, there is hope. God says that although the earth "will wear out like a garment; like clothing, he will change them and they will be changed" (Psalm 102:25-26). God is our hope for the restoration of all things (Acts 3:20-21).

The biblical story tells us that God has a place for humans in the future (John 14:1-3; Revelation 21:1-5). God's story is clear in saying that his people will rule with Christ Jesus in the next age of the world (Daniel 7:21-27; 2 Timothy 2:12; Revelation 5:9-10). Since his created humans have allowed evil into the world, he must now redeem and transform human lives, resurrect new bodies capable of living in tune with God's will, and restore the earth to a renewed goodness (Romans 8:18-25). Humans and the earth are connected and always shall be bound together in God's plan. There will be new heavens and a new earth, Christ will be king, humans will reign with Christ, and they will continue to fulfill their role of ruling over an earth that was made for them by God. It will be the fulfillment of what the Lord taught us to pray and what he demonstrated while on earth: "Thy kingdom come *on earth* as it is in heaven."

In other words, the rule and realm of God—what Christians under Christ's leadership have been living out from this present day until Christ comes again—will finally be completed. Christ, after defeating all evil, will then turn the kingdom over to God, who will rule over all, the visible and invisible (1 Corinthians 15:20-28). What we call heaven will include God's eternal, far-reaching spiritual dimension, God's eternal physical dimension, and maybe many more dimensions. Humans will continue to live on an earth and in a city of God, just as the Old and New Testaments have foretold and pictured for us. The material and immaterial will be joined, and both elements will make up heaven, the next age of the world for those who are in Christ Jesus. Unlike many on earth today who try to separate this world from God, the Bible and a true observation of nature corrects that thinking and unites all things. Scientists know by observation that physical things wear out; the sun is dying, and if all keeps going in that direction, the earth will die with it. Would allowing God to be part of the picture give people hope that is available nowhere else (Revelation 21:5)?

(4) THE STUDY OF NATURE REVEALS GOD

What we observe in our natural world will reveal something about the God who created it (Romans 1:20; Job 12:7-9; Psalm 19:1). For example, if you or I make something, and no one ever sees us, he or she will still be able to know something about the one who made it. When they observe it, they will know that it looks made, know that a mind was behind it, and know that whoever made it had artistic skills, a sense of symmetry and beauty, and so forth. In the same way, the Bible tells us that discovering things about God's creation reveals things about its maker. Although nature is not as explicit as the Bible in the information it gives, it reveals that the world was made by some great power that possesses qualities like a mind, creativity, beauty, orderliness, wisdom, eternality, love, and so forth. For example, love can be attributed to earth's maker by noticing all the ways the earth provides and cares for human needs.

What do scientific studies of our physical world reveal about God? Humans invented telescopes and microscopes that enable us to explore areas unseen by the naked eye, and we marvel at what we find. Seeing the vast endlessness of space reveals that the God of scripture may indeed be one who exists without end. Likewise, seeing the miniscule structure of living cells that make up the human body reveals unimaginable details. One of those details is that there exists information which is used to build the parts of the human body. Such a wealth of information in the cell reminds us of our human-made computers. The computer contains great amounts of information because the minds of humans programmed it; they put information into it. Similarly, the human cell contains lots of information, implying it was programmed by a mind.

After high school, I worked in a shop that rebuilt automobile starters and generators. I got the job because I attended a vocational high school, majored in automotive electricity, and learned how to make car repairs. When car parts wear out or break down, they do not fix themselves. Someone fixes them using information on how to do it. That information consists of words that someone put into automotive repair manuals. Where did the words in the manuals originate? Obviously, the information came from the mind of a person who figured things out. That information was transferred by physical means into a repair manual, thus making it visible so others could read it.

We could say that, on a human level, all the material things we make originate from ideas in minds that think, reason, and understand. For example, I recently got an idea for building a cabinet of shelves that my wife could use in the kitchen. The idea of how to do it originated in my mind, and I transferred it onto paper so my idea could be used in constructing the cabinet according to my specs. Apparently, that same process is at work in the human cell. There is information that tells the cell how to build human body parts. How did the information get there? By chance? Does it imply the existence of a mind that put the information in the cell to tell it what to do?

Scientists believe that the basic substance of this world is matter and energy. The origin of matter and energy is thought to be adequately explained through natural causes, such as the Big Bang, etc. Some scientists now propose *information* as a third foundational substance of the world. If information is a foundational part of this world, it again raises the question of origin. Some scientists are putting forth effort to find a natural explanation, meaning an explanation that does not need to include a personal God. The discovery of information in the biological cell raises interesting questions. What is information? Where does the information come from? If information does exist, what can we be led to believe? Interestingly, Francis Collins, from his involvement in the Human Genome Project, a scientific study of genetic material, was impressed by the information present in that material. From his observation of nature, he has written a book titled, *The Language of God*.

Many scientists have no problem believing in a God who is the source of our world and us. Other scientists are not willing to admit there is a mind outside of a physical universe that made it all. They believe it created itself, perhaps by chance over long ages of time. Although some scientists believe this, the more science discovers about how the world works, the more they discover what I have just tried to show with my car and shelf illustrations—that where we find information, we assume a mind at work. On a human level, we know that such information only comes from a being with a mind, not from the physical object itself.

Who *that mind* is cannot be known by human observation. Such observations only tell us that such a mind exists. That is why God has given us another book to help answer some of the questions raised by scientific discoveries. Besides the book of nature, we have the Bible, and in that book is revealed the originator of all things, the God who thinks, reasons, understands, creates what is visible, and then supplies what maintains it (Colossians 1:13-17). Unfortunately, humans have been successful in not allowing God to be a part of science. They prefer to say things like, "We know the world looks made, which implies a maker, but we must continue to remind ourselves that such a thing is not true. The world made itself." Unfortunately, Christians can also be guilty of attitudes that help create conflict between the Bible and science. Such attitudes result in the average person thinking Christians are against science and are unreasonable. And so, the battle between faith and science rages on.

PROPER ATTITUDES CAN BRING OPPOSING SIDES TOGETHER

Some of the attitude problems that stand in the way of bringing science and the Bible together have to do with the word *biased*. Christians are accused of being *biased* toward God and the Bible and therefore unwilling to listen to scientific proofs showing the Bible's Creation story to be untrue. That may be true, depending on the definition of *bias*. Everyone is biased. Being biased can be good or bad. When a person's bias bends them toward what is true and right, bias is good. What makes a bias bad is when a person refuses to hear the other side of an issue and hangs onto their own ideas and beliefs in the face of reasonable evidence against those beliefs.

Often, a person who is not open to other points of view is biased because of personal character defects. For example, refusal to listen to others may be due to a fear of knowing the truth, or a prideful need to be right, or stubborn willfulness, or dislike of another position, or dishonesty and self-seeking, or disbelief in God and his revelation of truth, or their preconceptions and misunderstandings of others' views, or even their own views. In such cases, a person will remain blind to the truth because, for some reason, they don't want to know it. A person is honest and has a good heart when, in the face of conflicting opposition, he or she wants to know the truth about how things really are and is willing to put forth an effort to seek the truth.

Both science and religion ought to be about finding the truth. When a scientist recognizes the unknown aspects of discoveries, understands how science works, and realizes that they may not yet have the final answer to their questions, they remain open-minded until their questions are answered. The same is true for Bible believers. They may not have the last word about what the Bible teaches. There is, however, nothing wrong with holding on to beliefs about subjects that are based on information known at the time. All of us believe things, right or wrong, based on how we see things at any given moment. The good scientist, the good Bible student, or anyone else will change their beliefs when they encounter new insight from reasonable and convincing evidence. This is what good scientists or Bible interpreters do if they possess a flexible bias—one open to new evidence.

For example, Antony Flew, an honest atheist who believed he had valid reasons for rejecting belief in the existence of God, was willing to change his mind when presented with further evidence. He believed in going where the evidence leads a person. What evidence convinced him to change? Among other things in his book *There Is a God*,[12] he mentioned two sufficient reasons for changing his views. One was scientifically discovered facts about DNA in living cells, and the second was arguments by N. T. Wright regarding the historical truth of the bodily resurrection of Christ Jesus. Openness to go where the evidence leads is what any person would do who honestly cares about what is true.

Another example of changing one's mind due to further information happened to biochemical scientist Michael Behe.[13] Trained in evolutionary science, he believed what he was taught

12. Antony Flew, *There Is a God: How the World's Most Notorious Atheist Changed His Mind* (New York: Harper One, 2007).
13. Michael J. Behe, *Darwin's Black Box: The Biochemical Challenge to Evolution* (New York: Free Press, 1996).

until presented with evidence that had not been presented in his former training. When faced with this new evidence, he considered it and eventually was convinced to change his mind about evolution. For one thing, he could not see how the Darwinian mechanism of natural selection, with small increments of change over a long time, could produce new living organisms when it seemed a fact that an organism needed all its vital parts functioning simultaneously to enable it to survive.

An example of Bible-believing Christians changing their mind about the created world happened when science discovered that the earth revolved around the sun rather than the sun around the earth. Christians believed the Bible taught that the earth was the center of the universe, and when science said differently, it created a huge battle between scientists and biblical scholars. In the end, science helped biblical students arrive at a better interpretation of scripture. It appears that God's book of nature and God's book of biblical revelation can influence each other toward the truth.

Yes, I am biased toward my faith, just as others are biased toward their beliefs. We all have a bent toward what we believe is real and true. I try not to be biased in the sense of refusing to consider opposing views, but to examine all sides and go where the evidence reasonably leads.

Understand, I am not saying a person needs to take an evidential scientific approach in order to experience a true and valid faith in God. Anyone can genuinely have a personal relationship with God by faith in God's Word and in Christ Jesus and by experiencing the transforming power of the Holy Spirit. In fact, one's personal experience of what God has done in his or her life can certainly be a valid reason for one's belief in God and a valid argument against any opposition. Furthermore, a person does not necessarily become a Christian by being convinced of certain arguments but rather through faith that believes and receives what Jesus offers (John 1:12-13).

A COMMENT ON INTERPRETING GENESIS 1

So what are we saying about the place of science in God's story of his earth? Science, through its discoveries, can provide a confirmation that the God of the Bible exists and cares about us. As some have expressed, "Seeing is believing," and God apparently provides a few sightings that bolster the faith of many or that help create a person's faith in God. Science can also be right in some of its observations that believers in Creation may not be willing to accept.

What is the place of faith in God's story of the earth? Christians need to continue to seek the right interpretation of scripture. I can think of seven interpretations of Genesis 1. Most of them are interpretations that try to make the Bible fit with the teachings of the science of evolution. They are based on the premise that evolution is true. But what if science discovers reasons to reject evolution? That would mean that those interpretations would no longer be necessary. Would those interpretations remain the same, or would they need to be changed? Both science and Bible interpreters need to keep pursuing truth as their goal.

Here is a brief account of one of those interpretations of Genesis 1, an interpretation of the Bible that is little known. The reader will have to investigate to see how valid it is when considering all available biblical and scientific data. This view attempts to show that the universe can be old, and a young six-day creation can be possible, thus potentially satisfying both old- and young-earth creationists.

Genesis 1:1 says, "In the beginning God created the heavens and the earth." The interpretation of this verse says God created the universe before he begins the six days. According to verse one, God's creation of the heavens means the stars, planets, galaxies, etc. Of all the planets, the focus centers on planet earth. According to verse 2, "The earth was formless and void, darkness was over the surface of the deep, and the Spirit of God was moving over the surface of the waters." Although created at the same time as the heavens, the earth was not yet made inhabitable for life. God made it into a biosphere, which means a planet built to sustain life. This was accomplished during the six-day Creation week in Genesis 1:3-31.

This interpretation differs from the interpretation that says verses 1 and 2 are simply an introduction and start to the Creation week, which continues in verses 3 and following. Theology professors Keil and Delitzsch, recognized scholars in the Hebrew language (now deceased), commented about Genesis 1:1 in their twenty-five-volume Old Testament commentary. Concerning Genesis 1:1, they wrote,

> *This sentence (Genesis 1:1) . . . is not a mere heading, nor a summary of the history of the creation, but a declaration of the primeval act of God, by which the universe was called into being. That this verse is not a heading merely, is evident from the fact that the following account of the course of the creation commences with "and" which connects the different acts of creation with the fact expressed in verse 1, as the primary foundation upon which they rest.*[14]

In other words, it is their view, based on the Hebrew use of language, that God created the universe in some form before the six-day Creation week began.

Since this interpretation is possible, then when God says in verse 3, "Let there be light" (since light was already created in verse 1), it means there may have been clouded conditions making the earth look dark to earth-bound observers. According to God's revelation to Job in Job 38:4, 7-9, when God first created the watery earth, it was apparently shrouded in cloud, making the earth a dark place. Thus when God commanded, "Let there be light," the atmosphere was cleared enough to let the light penetrate the darkness on the earth. This light could be likened to an experience I had when forest fires created a dense smoke in the atmosphere. I saw light coming through the murky sky, but the source of the light could not be seen. If Genesis 1 is an account, as if someone were observing it from their viewpoint on earth, it would appear to them that the darkness was overcome by light shining through.

According to a different interpretation of these verses, since the sun was not created until the fourth day of Creation week, this light in verse 1 had to come from another source. Some interpret this light in verse 1 as a divine light coming from God himself. The Bible does indicate that there are other light sources than the sun. It does seem odd to some, however, that God would not create the sun until the fourth day and creates the plants before their needed life

---

14. Carl Friederich Keil and Franz Delitzsch, *Commentary on the Old Testament* (Peabody, MA: Hendrickson Publishers, 1996).

source: the sun. Could it not have been possible to create the sun in the beginning as stated in verse 1?

The Bible does seem to say that God created the heavens' lights on the fourth day of Creation week, so how could Genesis 1:14-19 be interpreted if God created the heavens in verse 1 before Creation week began in verse 3? Could it be that God finished clearing the clouds away on the fourth day, making the sun and sky clear so that these heavenly bodies could be seen, and that God thus made visible for earth's observers the courses of these heavenly bodies to make for times and seasons?

Halley's Bible Handbook has had many editions, and remains a bestseller with millions of copies sold worldwide. This well-received handbook on the Bible says this: "The sun, moon, and stars must have been created in the beginning. On the 1st day their light must have penetrated the earth's mists (1:3), while they themselves were not visible. But now, due to lessened density of the clouds . . . they became visible on earth."[15] Some Hebrew scholars say the word *asah*, translated as "made" in some Bible versions, has a primary meaning of "to make a thing previously existing into something." Thus in Genesis 1:16 God made the pre-existing sun, moon, and stars to be timekeepers and lights on earth; on day four he made these visible, as it would look to observers on earth. Very few know of this interpretation, but it seems, according to Keil and Delitzsch, and Bible student Henry Halley, along with others, this interpretation has been around for a while.

CONCLUDING THOUGHTS

It is my understanding that the role of science is to discover by observation and experimentation the secrets of the natural world, how it works, and how we can use it to benefit and better our lives. God evidently designed the earth to be our habitation and sustainer of life, and to discover its hidden secrets is a part of his plan. Science is of great benefit to all of us, but it ought not to exceed its realm of operation. For example, science cannot say that the universe operates by certain natural laws and that no other laws outside of the natural

---

15. Henry H. Halley, *Halley's Bible Handbook* (Grand Rapids, MI: Zondervan, 1959).

realm exist. If there is a God, as the Bible reveals, then science must allow for signs of God within the natural world, even allowing that unusual or miraculous events can happen, though they do not fit the normal laws of nature. Science is here to say what is observed, not limit what could be possible given the existence of the God revealed in the Bible. The truth is that the more we discover in nature, the more God seems to show up. Nature will exhibit signs of God, which we can choose to see and believe or not. By biblical faith, and by scientific discoveries, we can know that God created the heavens and the earth. To overcome misinformation and misunderstandings, the facts must be allowed to speak for themselves—not our wishes or preferences due to personal belief or unbelief in God.

God wrote two books: nature and the Bible. The invisible realm of spirit and mind are connected with the physical world of matter and energy. The two belong together. It is sad when a scientific world that gives us so many good things to improve the quality of our lives tries to keep God out of it, as if he has nothing to do with us and the world we live in. The truth is that a correct understanding of both nature and the Bible will reveal that the two agree about what they say concerning our world. God's future age will continue to connect the invisible Spirit of God and his new physical earth together as one. It is Christ Jesus who demonstrates the spiritual and the physical as one, for he embodies both the invisible God from a spiritual heaven and the visible man from a physical earth.

CHAPTER 9

WE WALK BY FAITH AND NOT BY SIGHT

A friend once told me that he knew a missionary who was blind. Someone asked this missionary how he could accomplish all he has been doing for God without being able to see. The missionary's answer was, "I walk by faith and not by sight." That is one way to interpret this scripture verse, but what does it mean in its context?

The Apostle Paul is writing a letter to the people in the Corinthian church, telling them of his sufferings. He's been afflicted in every way, perplexed, persecuted, struck down, always carrying about in his body the dying of Jesus—but it has not defeated him. He does not lose heart. He is looking at the things of God that are eternal. Our sufferings are temporary (Romans 8:18). We have much to look forward to, for we walk by faith and not by sight—faith in something greater than our sufferings. What we see and experience daily is nothing compared to what our faith sees is ahead for us. Paul provides encouragement and comfort, for we all go through trying times. He is reminding believers about their faith and the promises of God.

In the middle of his reminder, he interrupts what he is going to say next with this thought: "For we walk by faith and not by sight" (2 Corinthians 5:7). That thought that entered his mind as a brief aside sums up what the Christian life is all about. Although Paul applies the statement to his current circumstances, it applies to many other situations as well, and the verse describes how we live as followers of Jesus in every situation of every day.

Physically speaking, to *walk* is how we move from one place to another, and we walk with a purpose, or aim, or destination in mind. Paul's address to Christians is to live each day of our journey by faith and not by sight. By using the words *faith* and *sight,* Paul is making a distinction between people who live with spiritual eyes on God and the things he has made known to them, as opposed to those who live with physical eyes set on the things of this world only. Those who live without faith in God have their eyes focused on the temporary things of this world. Those who live by sight are those who walk by their own senses, who live for the approval of others, who are influenced by their societal and cultural values, and who are without the hope God offers. They are people who are satisfied and rewarded only by the hopes, dreams, ambitions, pleasures, human-based religions, and good deeds of an earthly life. Followers of Jesus, on the other hand, have an eternal perspective and focus on what pleases God (2 Corinthians 5:9; 4:16-18). Their walk is from this world to another world, from this world to a world Christ is presently making and will complete when he comes to establish his eternal kingdom on the new earth. Following, we shall consider ways Christians walk by faith and not by sight.

(1) BELIEVE IN GOD'S EXISTENCE AND HIS BLESSINGS

We walk by faith and not by sight when we need God to save us from something bad in our lives, and we come to him, believing he exists and will reward those who seek him (Hebrews 11:6). The Apostle Paul, along with countless others, believed in something else before coming to faith in God's salvation. Paul did not believe in Jesus, and he was trying to destroy Christ's Church, thinking he was protecting the Jewish people from error. Paul came to a saving faith, based on Jesus appearing to him and telling him that his life was going in the wrong direction (Acts 26:12-18). We may not experience seeing Jesus as

Paul did, but at some point in our lives we get a similar message—a message that tells us our life is going in the wrong direction or is lacking something we need. We must believe God exists and trust him to save us, believing he is telling us the truth and will reward us with what we need. Faith means committing our lives to the one we believe will save us, even when we do not yet understand how that works or what may happen to us.

I remember when I first believed. I was terrified of death, and when I learned of Jesus, that those who believed in him would never die (John 11:25-26), I believed he existed and could save me. It was God who caused my heart to fear, creating in me the need and desire to be saved from what I feared. It was God who relieved my fear and my death by sending me his message of hope. It was like he sought me before I could seek him. Once I knew who he was and what he would do for me, I believed in him. It seems it was that way also for Paul. Jesus sought him to tell him he needed to change something in his life. Paul believed him and his life changed direction. What do you remember about the circumstances that caused you to come to God and believe in him, asking him to save you? We walk by faith and not by sight when we believe God exists and rewards with salvation and blessings those who receive him as savior. When we obey his call to save us, we enter an ongoing life of learning to walk by faith. (Galatians 2:20; Hebrews 11:6-16; Matthew 6:33; Mark 10:17-30; John 1:12-13; Ephesians 1:13-14).

(2) Overcome Trials and Focus on God's Promises

We walk by faith and not by sight when, in the midst of trials, afflictions, and sufferings, we believe God will work all things together for good to those who love him and are called according to his purpose (Romans 8:28-29). Walking by faith is especially important when faced with situations that threaten our well-being.

Joseph was a good example of this. His story is told in Genesis 37 and 39-50. God allowed bad things to happen to him, but Joseph maintained his walk of faith in God, even when unable to see how the bad could work out for good. His brothers sold him to merchants who were on the way to Egypt. It was an evil thing to do and very upsetting to Joseph (Genesis 42:21), but even though he may not have felt it at the time, God was with him (Acts 7:9). Joseph continued to live his life the way God wanted him to live it. For example, he said "no" to committing adultery with another man's wife, knowing it was a sin against God. Even though he obeyed God, he landed in prison for two years because of her false charges against him. However, he remained faithful to God, and in God's time, his circumstances resulted in becoming second-in-command over all of Egypt. He subsequently saved many people from starvation, including his family. By saving his family, God worked through Joseph to aid in his master plan of redeeming the world through Christ. Later, there came a day when Joseph was able to say to his brothers, "You meant evil" (by wanting to get rid of him), "but God meant it for good, to preserve many people alive" (Genesis 50:20). Joseph's example demonstrates that "God causes all things to work together for good to those who love God, to those who are called according to his purpose" (Romans 8:28). Even though we may not see how bad things that happen to us can work for good, we keep walking by faith.

A negative example is the nation of Israel. Israel, in bondage and hard labor under Egypt's rule, cried out to God to save them (Exodus 1:8-14; 2:23-25). God freed them through a series of miracles culminating in his parting of the Red Sea so they could escape Egypt's pursuing army. The Lord saved them that day from the Egyptians, and when they saw what God did, they believed in the Lord and in God's servant, Moses (Exodus 14:30-31). God promised them a land of their own, and he was now leading them there. However, when they entered the wilderness, they faced new trials and hardships. It was scary and worrisome. All the Israelites could do was focus on their problems and sufferings. For example, they had no water or food supplies to keep them alive, and they resorted to complaining and accusing Moses of bringing them out in the wilderness to die. They had said they believed in the Lord, but now they forgot what the Lord had promised them. He promised to lead them to a new land, but when God tested their hearts, they did not believe God's promise, acted on their own, and failed to listen to him and do what he said (Exodus 16:1-8). Instead of walking by faith in what God said or promised, when hardships came, they focused on the physical things they could see were bad for them, became afraid, and rebelled against the Lord. Thus, they were walking by sight and not by faith. They did not believe God would work all things for good to those he called to serve his purposes.

Day by day, as we renew our inner self through faith in things unseen and eternal, we overcome our trials and do not lose heart when God asks us to live our faith in the face of opposing circumstances. The Bible says to count it all joy when we encounter various trials, knowing that the testing of our faith produces endurance, and endurance will result in the fulfillment of God's good purposes for our lives (James 1:2-4). We walk by faith and not by sight when we overcome our trials, afflictions, sufferings, and fears by believing God will work all things together for good and fulfill his promises to bring us safely to the glorious destination he has promised us.

(3) Trust God's Providence

We walk by faith and not by sight when we make a decision that needs to be made and follow through with it, trusting God's providential workings (Proverbs 3:5-6). To walk by faith and not by sight involves two seemingly contradictory things. We are free to plan and choose our ways, guided by God's Word, and at the same time, God in heaven determines and directs our paths. The Bible tells us that both of these are at work simultaneously. "The mind of man plans his way, but the Lord directs his steps" (Proverbs 16:9). The story of Abraham's servant, in the matter of finding a wife for his master, is one example of this (Genesis 24:1-27). This principle of our will and God's will working together is also seen in the verse that says, "Work out your salvation with fear and trembling; for it is God who is at work in you, both to will and work for his good pleasure" (Philippians 2:12-13). Jesus illustrates this seemingly contradictory principle in that while he *voluntarily* chose to lay down his life on a cross, God had already *determined* the cross would be part of his plan. To walk by faith and not by sight means faithfully choosing to follow Christ Jesus, living by his example and teachings, while at the same time trusting God to direct our lives in ways that will fulfill his good will, both in our lives and in the lives of others.

Abraham's servant, as mentioned above, was walking by faith and not by sight when he followed God's directive to find a wife for his master. He was following what Proverbs 3:5-6 says to do: "Trust in the Lord with all your heart and do not lean on your own understanding. In all your ways acknowledge him, and he will make your paths straight." This means that every day, in everything we do, we can acknowledge that God is present with us, helping us achieve his purposes through our daily routines, and trust him to guide us in the plans we have for the day. We ask God to fill us with his Spirit so that in each daily activity we would say and do the things that would honor his name (Galatians 5:25). We ask God to help us when we are uncertain of what to do—not knowing what to expect, but trusting God will work his good will in our lives. We step out and do what we plan to do, not relying on our understanding and expectations but humbly acknowledging that God will be there for us. As we proceed in this way to walk by faith and not by sight, we may not see or be aware of his working in and through our lives, but at times, he will allow us to see him at work in ways we did not expect.

Here is a prayer I need to use more often in connection with daily decisions I make. Based on Proverbs 3:5-6, I pray, "Lord, I am doing what you say in this verse. I am choosing to do what I think is the way I should go. I am acknowledging you as the one who, because of your love for me, goes before me and guides what happens. For our good and your glory, I trust you to direct my path."

To give you an idea of how this works, I share the following example of one of the rare times I practiced this prayer. It has to do with a routine daily task. My wife and I needed our passports renewed for an upcoming trip. Rather than get professional help, our daughter showed me how to get applications from the internet and prepare everything ourselves. I planned to take it all to the post office the next day, but I was not sure I completed everything as needed, nor did I know the best way to mail them. Knowing that if things were not done correctly, this passport process could take longer, I asked God to be with me and help me get everything I needed to complete the task correctly. I also asked his Spirit to fill me so I might be Christ-like with any situation or people I might encounter.

At the post office, I planned to ask for help. When I arrived, the lobby was full of people, and the line stretched into the hallway. I could see this would take a long while, requiring patience. I noticed a rack of mailers at the other end of the lobby, so I walked through a host of people to get to the rack. After looking at the options, I still did not know what method of mailing to choose. The line was moving very slowly, and I was patiently waiting, not sure about where I was in line. Suddenly, the door next to me opened, and a kind woman asked if anyone needed help. Being right next to her, I said that I had a few questions and explained what I wanted to do. She looked at my applications, told me one more thing I needed to fill out, picked out the appropriate envelope for mailing, gave me an address label, and made sure I had the correct address. I went to a table in the hallway, got everything ready, and went to another post office where I promptly mailed them and left with joy, thanking and marveling at God for the unexpected and providential way he helped me.

Another example involves one of the ways God lets us know something he wants us to do. He allows us to see a need and then puts in our heart the desire to want to do something about it. For example, a person saw a need in his community for mentoring kids of single parents who were struggling to make life work. He had no idea of how to do it or where to begin, but he decided God wanted him to do it, so he trusted God to direct his way. Sometimes, we may hesitate to do what we believe God put into our minds to do because it looks impossible, we do not know how to do it, we doubt it will work, or we do not want to spend the time and money. However, we cannot see God at work and his kingdom come into the lives of people on earth if we do not risk stepping out in faith and doing things we believe he is asking us to do. We cannot let fear or doubt keep us from acting. When we see the needs of others and hear God prompting us to do something, we need to risk stepping out in faith to do what God wants. The prayer I stated above applies here: "Lord, I am doing what I believe you want me to do. I am choosing to do what I think is the way to do it. I am acknowledging you as the one who goes before me and guides what happens. For our good and your glory, I trust you to direct my path."

The man who wanted to start a mentoring ministry for kids trusted God, and God did some amazing things. One of the things the man had to do was recruit people to be mentors to the kids. He wasn't sure how to get contacts, when one day, the priest of the Catholic church in town called and asked him to come and present the need during a regular worship service. As a result, many from the church volunteered to be mentors. In the end, a number of churches became involved, a training program for volunteers was established, and the community had a mentoring program for one-parent kids.

There are, of course, other times God, by his providence, shows he is with us, even without us asking for help. I will share a story that I am sure will remind you of your own stories about when you experienced a similar providential work of God.

We were moving from Montana to Michigan and needed our GPS to help us get around in our new surroundings. Somehow, the cord that plugged our GPS into the car's electrical outlet was missing. We searched everywhere and even tried various cords from phones and other electronic devices. Nothing worked. We were ready to leave town when a friend walked in to say goodbye and to give us a parting gift. Having no idea of our problem, she supplied us with a GPS identical to the one we had, and now we had the cord we needed.

We never know when God will show up, or how things will work out in our daily walk with him. We make our plans, but God directs and has the last word. We give him freedom to open or close the door. We walk by faith and not by sight when we make a decision that needs to be made, follow through with it, and trust God's providential workings.

(4) OBEY GOD'S WILL

We walk by faith and not by sight when we obey God's revealed will, believing that by doing so we are bringing something of God's kingdom on earth as it is in heaven. To walk by faith, and be more effective in serving God's cause, it helps us to know God's overall plan for his world, including his plan for us as his people. We learn this through his story told in the Bible. Knowing his story, we become aware of the part he wants us to play, and we aim our prayers at seeking his kingdom and asking his help in doing what he wants us to do. As we go about living as he wants and loving as he loves, he will work through us to make our daily lives a contribution to his overall plan. By doing his will each day, we will fulfill our part in his marvelous story of redeeming the world as we help his kingdom to come on earth as it is in heaven.

We see a modern-day example of walking by faith and not by sight in the life of Mother Teresa, who lived out her life serving the needs of the poor in the slums of Calcutta, India. Letters she wrote reveal that much of her life serving God and loving people was lived with a feeling that she was alone and God had abandoned her. Yet with faith, she prayed daily, and even when she was not aware of God's presence, she kept on with her work, doing what she knew God had called her to do. She may not have seen what God was doing through her, but the results of her work following her death have been ongoing and will likely become even more meaningful when Jesus comes to complete his kingdom on earth as it is in heaven (Matthew 6:9-10). To walk by faith and not by sight is to believe that God is working in and through our daily lives to accomplish his purposes, even though we may not see it or feel it. To walk by faith and not by sight means that no matter how bad things in this world appear to be, our faith in God gives us courage to keep walking in ways that are pleasing to him.

Jesus did the will of his father when he fed the hungry, helped heal people, forgave the guilty, raised people from death to life, spread the truth, took care of his family, and lived a life morally pleasing to his father. By obeying the things God sent him to do, Jesus was showing us, in some measure, what the future kingdom of God will be like. Likewise, by doing God's will and good works, we too will be bringing something of God's kingdom on earth (Matthew 25:34-40). Then, one day, when Jesus comes again, we will find that the things we have done, no matter how small, contributed to the final completion of God's plan for a new and evil-free world. As we learn to walk by faith and not by sight, God will fulfill his plans in us and through us. We walk by faith and not by sight when we obey

God's revealed will, thus bringing something of God's kingdom on earth as it is in heaven.

(5) PASS THROUGH DEATH WITHOUT FEAR

We walk by faith and not by sight when we come face to face with the door of death, realizing we are about to pass through to the other side. Fear of death is a common human emotion (Hebrews 2:14-15). Often we may face health conditions that threaten our lives. The Apostle Paul says that when we are burdened excessively, beyond our strength, despairing even of life, "We have the sentence of death within ourselves so that we would not trust in ourselves, but in God who raises the dead" (2 Corinthians 1:8-9). Our hope is in God's promised deliverance (1 Corinthians 6:14). We can, with confidence, look forward to death as ushering us into the presence of our beloved Jesus. To be absent from the body is to be at home with the Lord (2 Corinthians 5:8).

If we experience feelings of fear when facing death, we need to be reassured of our faith. I visited an elderly lady in the hospital who said she was afraid to die because of her sins. She was a believer in Christ, but just before her death, she had doubts. I quoted 1 Peter 2:24 to her that says, "He himself [Jesus] bore our sins in his body on the cross." Through hearing his Word, she was reassured that her sins were forgiven and was enabled to die in peace.

It can also give us peace in the face of death to review some of the promises we have waiting for us on the other side of that door. It is a place Jesus has been preparing for us (John 14:1-3). It is a place where there is no more sickness, pain, suffering, death, and crying (Revelation 21:4). It is a place free of all evil, guilt, and worry, where only righteousness, peace, and joy are found (Romans 14:17). It is a place where we are together with all other believers (1 Thessalonians 4:16-17). It is a place where we will live in resurrected and perfect bodies, like Jesus's body (Philippians 3:20-21). It is a place where heaven and earth are made new and will undoubtedly be much like our present earth, complete with beauty and things to discover and do (Romans 8:19-23; Psalm 102:26-27; 2 Peter 3:13; Matthew 5:5). It is a place where we will discover the many things God has prepared for us that are beyond our imagination (1 Corinthians 2:9).

Like Jesus, who committed his life into God's hands when he was on the cross (Luke 23:46), our surrender might sound like this: "Lord, if it is my time to be with you, it is OK. I know I will be present with you in your heavenly realm and that my body will be resurrected unto eternal life through the power of your Spirit who resides within me" (Romans 8:11). On this side of death's door, faith in our promised hope from God can bring peace, excitement, and joy in what we are about to experience. Being ready to enter his unseen glory by surrendering our life into the hands of God is to live by faith and not by sight. The Lord Jesus is our Good Shepherd. He loves his sheep and will lead us only to good places that will completely satisfy us. When we answered the call to believe in Jesus, we entered his kingdom here on earth, where we live by faith and not by sight. When our corruptible body dies, that is when the kingdom of God in all its promised fullness and sight begins, and we will dwell in the house of the Lord forever (Psalm 23).

CHAPTER 10

FAITH AND PRAYER

It would be hard to argue against the idea that faith is perhaps most used in the practice of prayer. The Bible says that if you ask something from God, ask in faith without doubting (James 1:6). In putting this book about *faith* together, I seriously thought a chapter on prayer should be the first chapter, but with further thought, I believe ending the book with a chapter on prayer is most fitting. As some have said, "Having the last word is perhaps the most remembered and the most impactful." I sense an "lol" from God when I compare the decision to put prayer last to Jesus's words, "The first shall be last and the last first" (Matthew 19:30). I am putting prayer last in the book to emphasize that prayer should be first in our lives. Books and books have been written about prayer, and I cannot possibly say enough to adequately cover such a huge subject. I will be happy if I can simply help readers want prayer to be more a part of their walk with God and provide motivation for them to do something about it.

I don't know about you, but I feel my prayer life is quite lacking. I have questions about prayer, and for a long time, I have wanted my prayer life to be better. Although I talk to God throughout the day, which is a form of prayer, the thought has often bothered me that I should pray more and do a better job of praying for others. As a Christian, my lack of prayer is especially convicting whenever I read Bible verses like, "With all prayer and petition pray at all times in the Spirit, and with this in view, be on the alert with all perseverance and petition for all the saints" (Ephesians 6:18). Another convicting verse says, "Far be it from me that I should sin against the Lord by ceasing to pray for you" (1 Samuel 12:23).

Even though prayer has been a part of my life, it has not been what I know it could be. What is the problem? Do I not care? Do I have unanswered questions or doubts about prayer that make me skeptical? Am I too busy? One thing I have realized is that, when asked to pray for a particular need, I oftentimes do not know how to pray. What is prayer, really? How does it work, and why? What motivates us to pray? Is it only about asking God for things when we are in trouble? If prayer is so important, why don't we spend more time doing it? Is there anything we can do to help our prayers be more effective or to see them answered more frequently? Does prayer work?

Prayer as a link to God is one of life's great mysteries. Many years ago, the wife of a good friend of mine had taken their children swimming at a lake twenty miles from home. She removed a contact lens from her eye to clean it when the wind blew it out of her hand and into the water. Their family was scraping by financially, and contact lenses were very costly. She diligently and frantically searched a long while before finally giving up and returning home. She told her husband what happened, and seeing how upset she was, he said they would go back the next day and look for it. With a sense of earnestness and need, he prayed that God would help them find it. The next day, his wife pointed out the area where they were swimming, and as they began searching, an object suddenly appeared in the water, like a silver dollar brilliantly flashing in the sunlight. They went to it, picked it up from the bottom of the lake, and to his amazement, and against all odds, it was her contact lens. My friend shared with me that this experience with prayer caused him to believe in God in a new and deeper way. He said he was a nominal Christian but became more serious about his relationship with God because this answer to his prayer made a distant God real to him.

I know what some would say about such prayer experiences. Skeptics would doubt that God was involved. They would point out that people find lost items every day and do not need God and prayer to help them. They would say that our own minds tell us where to look and that not giving up finally pays off. I can understand skepticism, for I too have been tempted to think such things. However, another voice speaks into my life that I take more seriously than the skeptic's voice. The voice of Jesus has a different view of prayer. The disciples who daily lived with him saw him deeply involved in prayer, often taking time away from his busy activities to pray to his Father in heaven (Mark 1:35; Luke 5:15-16; 6:12; 9:18; 11:1). What motivated him to pray? What did prayer do for him? The disciples seemingly concluded that the love and power he exhibited must have something to do with his connecting with God through prayer. It prompted them to say to him, "Lord, teach us to pray" (Luke 11:1). Seeing their interest in prayer, Jesus did not hesitate to teach them. Thankfully he did, for we too can benefit from his teaching.

In chapter two, we emphasized that the Bible is the story of God. When we understand God's story and how he is at work to save his estranged world, we see that we, his people, have a part in making that happen. I would like to suggest that the prayer Jesus taught us to pray (Matthew 6:9-13) should be set in the context of his salvation story. It is a prayer to honor God and to ask him for the things we need in order to accomplish our part in his story. There are things we need from him every day if we are to help bring his kingdom on earth and do his will as it is in heaven.

Do you want to see God at work in your life and your prayers answered? In the context of living life for him and doing the works God wants us to do, Jesus clearly says, "Whatever you ask in My name, that will I do, so that the Father may be glorified in the Son. If you ask Me anything in My name, I will do it" (John 14:13-14). In our call to bear fruit for God, the same promise is made: "Ask whatever you wish, and it will be done for you" (John 15:7). What we have traditionally referred to as the Lord's Prayer, or the "Our Father," is not about asking God for what *we want*, it's about communing with God and asking God for what *we need* so that we can do what *he wants*. I like a definition of prayer credited to Alvin L. Reid. His definition is this: "Prayer is intimacy with God that leads to the fulfillment of his purposes."

It seems impossible for God to bring his *kingdom on earth as it is in heaven* in light of his choosing to work through imperfect, sin-infected, and self-willed humans. Yet working through such people in making that happen is how he chooses to operate. Therefore, in order for God's will to be done in and through us who are his beloved, trusted friends and voluntary servants, we must learn to get our sinful side out of the way so his good will and plan to save people can be accomplished. Thankfully, God *is at work* in us—to want what he wants so that his salvation plan can progress, first in us, and then from us to the world around us.

In order to be co-laborers with God in his work, we as his new creation in Christ must rely on him for all we need to get the job done. We need a faith life that seeks to put his kingdom and righteousness first, ahead of our self-will and ways (Matthew 6:33). Understand, I am not recommending we give up everything to serve God. I am only saying that his work be foremost in our desires and woven into our normal and daily lifestyles. Everything we do, whether it is raising our kids, working our daily jobs, engaging in social life, going to school, or enjoying the world God made for us, shall be done to fulfill our part in God's story. By repenting of our rebellious or straying ways and choosing to be healed by his love, we can become fruitful branches and lights to illumine God's way for people in a dark world in need of hope and a savior.

The key for us to be good representatives and workers for God is to daily, and often moment by moment, rely on the Lord's presence, wisdom, guidance, and power. Our primary way to make this happen is to remain in continuing, close communion with our heavenly Father, and that is what something we call *prayer* is all about. Once we have experienced God's salvation in our lives, prayer becomes the way we maintain our awareness of the presence of God, have our daily needs met, and humbly keep self-will out of the way so that his healing and saving ways can be done in and through us. We shall now survey the meaning of the prayer Jesus taught us to pray as a way to enable us to fulfill our part in his story.

THE PRAYER JESUS TAUGHT US TO PRAY

"Our Father" is not a request; rather, it is an approach to God in prayer with the understanding of who he is and who we are in

relationship to him. Knowing him as *"Our Father"* is the basis for being able to come to him and to ask him for things—not for things as if he is a magic genie who is there to grant all our wishes, but to meet those needs that will enable us to fulfill his purposes for our lives. For example, "Father, help me love this person right now," or, "Father, I need your wisdom in this situation."

Rather than give *"Our Father"* a quick greeting, we pause long enough to begin prayer with an inner sense of who God is and of his presence in our lives. We realize our dependence on him, not only for life itself but for everything we need that enables us to enjoy life and to do his will. Jesus, as our example, never did anything apart from wanting to please God and do the Father's will. In order to see God's purposes fulfilled in his life, Jesus spent much time in the presence of God to commune with him and to hear from him. In Acts 2:25, David tells us how Jesus related to the Father. Jesus said, "I saw the Lord always in My presence; for he is at my right hand, so that I will not be shaken." That can be true of us. For Jesus, and us, communion with God means being in the presence of the Father and sensing that life will be all right because God is with us.

Moses was charged with a part in God's salvation plan. He was to lead God's people out of slavery and into the Promised Land. It was an overwhelming task, and he said to God that he would and could not do it unless God's presence was with him (Exodus 33:12-16). We may not always realize God's presence, but we can pause anywhere, at any time, and repeat the words *"Our Father,"* and those words can instantly bring us into that awareness and mindset. Unless God is with us, we cannot achieve his ways and accomplish his goals. It is as Jesus once said, "Apart from Me you can do nothing" (John 15:4-8). As we abide in him and allow his words to abide in us, we experience the presence of *our Father* as a prelude for receiving the help we need to do his will.

"Hallowed be your name" is a continuation of addressing him as *"Our Father."* God has many names in the Bible. We can address him with other names that describe who he is. We can say, "Our Shepherd," "Our Healer," "Our Righteousness," "Our Lord," etc. and dwell for a few moments on what each of his names mean. After becoming aware of God's presence and addressing his name(s), our

initial request in this prayer is for his name to be hallowed. *Hallow* means to sanctify, to set apart, to make holy, to honor. Each of his many names reveals something different about what God is like and what he does. As beloved children of our Father, we hallow his name by honoring him. Desiring his name to be hallowed means that we do not profane his name by wrongdoing. (See Isaiah 29:22-23; Jeremiah 34:12-16.) We are to respect and represent the meaning of his name to the world around us. If his name is Righteous, and he gives us his righteousness, we are to live that way. If his name is Shepherd, and he is our Shepherd, we are to yield to his leadership. This is to hallow his name; otherwise, we take the name of the Lord in vain (Exodus 20:7). We can spend a few minutes at the beginning of this prayer thinking about the meaning of his name and how his name affects our lives. We can ask him to help us hallow his name by honoring him in the way we live in the presence of those who observe our behaviors.

"Your kingdom come, your will be done, on earth as it is in heaven." When Jesus Christ our Lord lived among us, he showed us what God's kingdom is like and will be like. Jesus fed the hungry, taught the ignorant, visited and comforted the hurting, healed diseases and deformities, demonstrated power over nature, had compassion on people's lack of direction, and raised the dead. He gave hope to those who had none. God's kingdom involves the elimination of all that is evil. Jesus gave us a taste of what God's kingdom on his new earth will be like (Revelation 21:4-5). He loved us in all these ways because of his love for God the Father, and he did nothing apart from the Father's will. Jesus did all these good works to show us the kind of world God has always intended his creation to be.

Jesus teaches us to pray for God's kingdom to come on earth as it is in the realm of his glory. We are to pray that his kingdom come and his will be done through us who are his people. A sample of our praying this part of the prayer might sound like this: "Lord, in order that people might see what your kingdom is like, help us do works like Jesus did in bringing his kingdom on earth. Help us convey to others the hope we have to one day see the glory of your kingdom fulfilled through Jesus when he returns to earth."

We have often missed seeing prayer as asking God to give us what we need to fulfill the work of his kingdom. Prayer is not so much to be self-focused as it is to be God-focused. Prayer is for help to do his will, not our will. Is that not the purpose of the prayer Jesus taught his disciples to pray? Jesus connects our praying to the work of his kingdom (John 14:12-14). When we ask God for whatever we need in order to accomplish his work, he will give us what we ask. The reason we pray for our families, our communities, our workplaces, our churches, our world, and ourselves is for God to fulfill his purposes through us in each of these areas. Jesus's whole life was lived to see the glory of God fulfilled, and that is our purpose as well. We pray for God to give us what we need to help bring his kingdom of love and goodness into each area of our life. Jesus said, "Apart from Me you can do nothing" (John 15:7). He meant that without his presence and power, we can do nothing to bring forth the fruit of God in our lives and in our world (John 15:1-8; Galatians 5:17-23).

Doing the work of God's kingdom is how we are being transformed into the likeness of Christ Jesus our Lord (Romans 8:29; Galatians 4:19; Ephesians 2:10; 5:1-2). We are beginning to bring his kingdom on earth when, like him, we visit the sick, feed the hungry, help the poor, lift the downtrodden, and love all people by seeking to meet their needs. When we share God's story and message of salvation, people can be raised to new life. We know that evil will only be totally overcome when Jesus comes to be the king of all peoples. May he come quickly, for the need is overwhelming and the evils of this world often seem to win. Remember God's word to us: we are not to be overcome by evil, but to overcome evil with good (Romans 12:21).

"Give us this day our daily bread" (Matthew 6:11). This part of the prayer is more important than we know. The power of evil within us and in this world is destroying us, which is why everything is dying. This prayer is asking for what we need from God to overcome evil so that the righteousness of God rules. Jesus knew that our daily bread was not only physical food but included every word that comes from the mouth of God. Jesus did the work of the Father, or it could be said that the Father did his work through the Son. Jesus always did the will of the Father (John 5:17-19, 30; 6:38; 14:10). He knew from God's Word what his Father wanted him to do. He relied on the Father for what he needed to enable him to do God's work.

God has also called each believer in Christ to have a part in bringing God's salvation plan to fulfillment (John 14:12). We too rely on God's Word, remembering "that man does not live by bread alone, but man lives by everything that proceeds out of the mouth of Lord" (Deuteronomy 8:3; Matthew 4:4). Jesus instructs us, "If My words abide in you, ask whatever you wish, and it will be done for you" (John 15:7). That being the truth, the food we ask for each day is not only physical food to strengthen our body but what we need spiritually to enable us to do his will and perform his work. The importance of this prayer is that evil can overtake us anytime and will do so if we are not on guard. Asking God each day to give us what we need to combat evil is vital.

Before proceeding, I know there are people who would say I am being too negative in emphasizing evil so strongly. They would argue that there are good people in the world and that there is much goodness. I am not denying that. Goodness in the world keeps us from becoming depressed, going crazy, and falling into despair and hopelessness. Goodness is why we fight against evil, but unless we recognize the depths of evil and what it takes to win against it, we shall be defeated. We cannot defeat evil without the help of goodness, and I am not talking about human goodness. Reliance on divine goodness is our only hope of victory (1 John 5:4). If we could do it ourselves, the world would be able to eliminate all laws, and families would be able to raise their kids without having to make any rules. The Bible is right; we are in a battle between good and evil. Because humans cannot eliminate the evil within themselves, it cannot be eliminated in the world. Only God can save us and make the world good again, and that is what he is doing. In his plan, he chooses people who will have faith in him, who are allowing him to change them, and who will cooperate with him in restoring all goodness through the Lord Jesus Christ. Christ wants to bring the kingdom of God on earth. Christ wants God's good will to be done.

For most of us, prayer has been a way to get God's help for our personal concerns—my health, my kids, my problems, my wants, my needs. There is no doubt that prayer is an invitation from God to ask anything of him, and it is not wrong to ask things for ourselves, for he is our heavenly Father who cares for us (Hebrews 4:16). Quite a bit of confusion has occurred over some of God's prayer promises, particularly those where Jesus says that if we ask anything in his name, he will do it (1 John 5:14-15; Matthew 7:7; 21:20-22). The confusion comes to us when we ask, believing God will grant our requests, but it does not happen as we want. Perhaps we need to realize that the prayer the Lord is teaching us does not begin with me asking God for what I want and need. The prayer begins with wanting to honor God and asking for what he wants.

Prayer needs a background of knowing God and his word to us. Often in our praying, we pray for what we want; but do we pray for what God wants? The Apostle Paul's prayer for all believers is that we "may be filled with the knowledge of his will in all spiritual wisdom and understanding" (Colossians 1:9-10). To grow in being able to pray effectively, we need to grow in our knowledge of who God is and what he desires for his world and for us. We must be open to hear from him, and one of the best sources for hearing from God is his word to us in the scriptures. When I know him, his ways, and his will, with spiritual wisdom and understanding, I can conform my prayers to what I know is his will.

Isn't that what Jesus means when he says things like, "If you ask Me anything in My name, I will do it" (John 14:14)? *In my name* means "according to who I am." John reminds all Christians in 1 John 5:14-15, "This is the confidence which we have before Him, that, if we ask anything according to His will, He hears us. And if we know that He hears us in whatever we ask, we know that we have the requests which we have asked from Him." The Bible also says that the Holy Spirit intercedes for us, according to the will of God (Romans 8:26-27). If the Holy Spirit prays according to the will of God, and God hears his prayers for us, how much more effective will our prayers be if we learn to pray according to the will of God? Where do we learn the will of God if not from the scriptures? Who wrote the scriptures? Are they not all inspired, or God-breathed, by God's Spirit? Our job, then, is to see if God says or promises anything in the Bible about what we are to pray for, then include those things in our prayers.

Knowing who I am in Christ leads me to realize God's purposes for my life. According to God's Word, we have become part of his people so that we "may proclaim the excellencies of him who has called [us] out of darkness into his marvelous light" (1 Peter 2:9). We proclaim his excellencies by developing and exemplifying his loving and righteous character in the ways we live, by enjoying his many good gifts, including his material world, as he meant for them to be enjoyed, and by sharing his message of forgiveness and new life in Christ. Each of us has become a new "creation in Christ," which in part means we are becoming conformed to the image of Jesus, God's Son (2 Corinthians 5:17; Romans 8:29). Motivated by his love, I no longer live for myself but for him who died and rose again on our behalf (2 Corinthians 5:15). As the psalmist said, "Not unto us, O Lord, not to us, but to Your name give glory because of Your lovingkindness, because of Your truth" (Psalm 115:1). Unfortunately, in this world of evil, pain and suffering are also a part of what we must experience in the process of achieving God's purposes for our lives and world (Mark 10:28-30; John 16:33; Philippians 3:7-11; 1 Peter 1:6-9; 2:19-23).

Here are a few questions to ask ourselves that may lead to the fulfilment of God's purposes:

1. How does prayer for my health fit in with God's will and purpose?

2. How does prayer for my marriage help in the fulfilment of God's will and purposes?

3. How does prayer for my kids help fulfill God's will and purposes?

4. How do prayers for my community, the world, my job, the church, and others help fulfill God's purposes?

5. Why do I pray for each of these areas and the people involved?

6. Does what I pray come out of communion with God and knowing his will and purpose?

Are we not to be concerned about our personal needs or wants? Jesus said that if we lose our lives for his sake, we find them. By seeking God's kingdom and his righteousness, things we need will be given us (Matthew 6:33). God will likely also throw in some other good gifts. He loves us and wants to give great gifts to us. All our desires will be met in the world to come, but in this world, they are met through seeking first his kingdom and his righteousness. For any situation we get into each day, we need something from God to help us do the right thing. For example, "God, give me your Spirit of love to love my neighbor," or, "Give me the wisdom I need to discipline my child as you would want," or, "Give me the attitude at work to love and serve others by meeting their needs through this job you have given me."

"Forgive us our debts, as we also have forgiven our debtors" (Matthew 6:12). We are not only to seek God's kingdom but also his righteousness (Matthew 6:33). This prayer's closing requests have to do with God's righteousness. His kingdom of righteousness, among other things, consists of unity, peace, and oneness in love. Practicing forgiveness is one of the ways his righteousness is achieved. Jesus taught us to love each other, even to love our enemies. Unity, peace, and love are threatened by disharmony, wrongs committed, resentments, anger, hatred, and ill-will toward self and others. Forgiveness enables the restoration of love and unity to broken relationships. Forgiveness is something we both give and receive. It involves forgiving others, forgiving self, and asking others to forgive us. There is need for us to learn how to do it.

In this part of the prayer for Christ's followers, he is assuming that people who are asking God's forgiveness will be people who forgive others, as God in Christ has forgiven them (Ephesians 4:32; Colossians 3:12-13). The truth is, there are opportunities to practice forgiveness toward self and others every day. When we think about it, how often do we ask and receive God's forgiveness, and how many people are there in our lives that need forgiveness? Forgiveness needs to become part of our daily lifestyle. Forgiveness has the power to heal all of us of our wrongs, our guilt, our shame, and our brokenness.

Jesus showed us something about the power of forgiveness through an event recorded in the Bible. He was a dinner guest at a Jewish religious leader's home when a woman entered and humbly showed Jesus her awesome respect and love. She fell at his feet, and with tears streaming from her eyes, she anointed his feet with perfume. The Jewish man, a Pharisee, was shocked and thought to himself that Jesus must not know who this woman was, or he would not have received such actions from her. The Pharisee was judging and condemning her, for he knew her to be a sinful, immoral woman of the streets. Jesus turned to the man and said, "Her sins, which are many, have been forgiven, for she loved much; but he who is forgiven little, loves little." Then he reaffirmed to the woman, "Your sins have been forgiven. Your faith has saved you; go in peace" (Luke 7:36-50).

Consider what Jesus was teaching us. Being forgiven sets a person free from their past life, free to start over and live a new life. The amazing and undeserved love a person feels from being forgiven restores their dignity and elevates their sense of being a person of worth. More than that, the deeper their guilt and pain from a damaged and ruined life, the more love they have for their forgiver, and the more love they have for others because they identify with others' pain and need for healing. Forgiveness transforms them into people who become free to love. Jesus was saying to the Pharisee that his lack of love meant he needed to be forgiven for his judgmental and condemning spirit, thus freeing him to love others. As long as the Pharisee thought he was all right and did not need forgiveness, the less likely it would be for him to experience the goodness of being part of God's righteous kingdom.

Not only do we learn about forgiveness from the teachings of Christ Jesus, we also learn about forgiveness from our personal experiences. A friend and I worked many days and long hours to fix up a building we owned that sat in a wooded area alongside a river. We used this building for kids' camp outings and adult retreats. One day I went there to do some maintenance and discovered the locked door had been forced open. When I went in, the place was in ruin. Sheetrock walls had holes punched in them, dishes from cupboards were scattered and broken, beer cans and messes were everywhere. Apparently, a drinking party took place by a group that had no respect for other people's property. I was more than angry at whoever did this. I wanted to find them and see them punished. I could not sleep at night. My anger was consuming me.

One night, while lying in bed, I planned ways to rig a gun so the next time they broke in, the gun would go off and shoot them. At that moment, unexpectedly, a voice entered my head and I heard, *Wait a minute. I thought you were a Christian, and you are planning to kill someone?* A scripture entered my mind that says, "'Vengeance is Mine, I will repay,' says the Lord." *You need to forgive them.* I knew that was true. Soon after that, I began wondering what their lives were like. Did they have a horrible home life, did bullying occur that made them angry at the world? Did they feel unloved? Then I said, "God, I forgive them for wrecking my property. If you want them punished, I turn that over to you, for you have said, 'Vengeance is mine, I will repay'" (Romans 12:19).

After I forgave them, I had thoughts and feelings like, *If I could get to know who did this, I would want to help them instead of hurt them.* The next night, my angry feelings returned, and I wanted to punish them all over again. Instead, I asked myself, *Didn't you forgive them? Yes, I did, just last night. Was your forgiveness genuine? Yes, it was. I sincerely wanted to forgive them.* So I reaffirmed my forgiveness and those thoughts and feelings never returned. We never did know who the guilty persons were, and it no longer mattered, except we hoped they did not continue such behavior and wreck other people's property, and we wished they could be changed by God's love.

I learned many things about forgiveness from this incident. I learned that if I don't forgive, I only hurt others and myself through self-destructive attitudes. I learned that it helps to forgive if you can think about others differently and develop sympathy for them. I learned that in cases where you cannot have contact with those who hurt you, you can still forgive them for your own sake, and that if you ever did have contact with those who hurt you, you would want to help them. I learned that forgiveness is talking to God, naming people who hurt you, telling God the specific thing(s) they did to harm you, and then saying to God that you forgive them. I learned that I was offending God by not forgiving because he had forgiven me. I learned that forgiving does not mean it will never enter your mind again, but that if it does, you reaffirm your forgiveness. I learned that you know if you have truly forgiven someone if you have feelings of wanting to help them and not hurt them. I learned that it costs to forgive. I had to suffer the cost of what they did, while they went free. This is not to say they should not have had to pay, but in this situation of not knowing who they were, there was no way to have justice. I learned forgiveness does not mean letting others get away with wrongs, but in this case, I learned that it helps to forgive if you can let go of your need for justice and let God perform the justice. I learned too that forgiveness does not always happen in an instant. It involves a needed and sometimes lengthy process to get us to the place of being willing to forgive.

Forgiveness is not easy to do. In order to do it effectively, there is much to learn. Sadly, forgiveness is rarely practiced by most people in their normal course of daily living, including Christians. If you are interested, there are many helpful books on this subject from a Christian perspective.[16] Lacking information about forgiveness is one reason we don't forgive. Other reasons include things like fear, justified anger, and pride. Faith in Christ's forgiveness is a key to practicing forgiveness. From him and his ongoing forgiveness of our lives, we receive the motivation and courage to enable us to forgive as he did. We have all experienced messed-up relationships and must assume some degree of responsibility in making things right. The only way relationships between us and God, and us and others, can be corrected is through practicing God's forgiving ways. When people hurt us, it is a reminder that we often hurt God and others by our wrongs and are continuously in need of receiving his forgiveness and thanking him for his mercy and love. How we forgive others demonstrates how we have been forgiven by God. Forgiveness saves us and helps create the kind of unified and loving world God wants. So we pray, "Thy kingdom come, thy will be done, through us."

"Do not lead us into temptation, but deliver us from evil" (Matthew 6:13). This last request, also involving righteousness, has to do with temptation and protection from evil. What does this prayer mean? *"Do not lead us into temptation"* is a difficult prayer to understand. Does it mean we are asking God not to lead us into temptation to sin? No! God does not tempt us to sin. Scripture says, "God cannot be tempted

---

16. Here are two practical books on forgiveness that have helped me. (1) Frank Desiderio, *Can You Let Go of a Grudge? Learn to Forgive and Get On with Your Life* (Mahwah, NJ: Paulist Press, 2014). (2) Doris Donnelly, *Putting Forgiveness into Practice* (Allen, TX: Argus Communications, 1982).

by evil, and he himself does not tempt anyone" (James 1:13). We are tempted to sin when carried away and enticed by our own lusts (James 1:14).

Here is an example. When I was a young boy, I was earning money to buy a baseball glove. I was short of my goal by a few dollars. I knew where my parents kept a money jar full of change. I stole a little from it to make up the amount I needed. My inward lust wanted what I wanted *now*, instead of waiting and earning it the right way. Another source of temptation to sin comes from others. Some boys I hung out with in my neighborhood wanted me to go with them to steal goods from a nearby store. In this case, I went home and did not give in to the temptation.

Here are a couple other examples of temptations to sin. Temptations to commit sins of sexual misconduct are rampant in our world. Such misconduct means to abuse others by raping them, whether physically or mentally, or it involves seeking other forms of sexual misconduct to achieve personal pleasure and self-gratification. God's good gift of sexual desire is to be fulfilled in right ways, ways he specifically defines in his Word. Yet another temptation to sin is to seek popularity or fame by pleasing people in order to gain acceptance, respect, a positive self-image, and feelings of security. People become our gods. Although wanting a positive image is not a bad thing, we need to realize that our ultimate identity, well-being, and safety comes from God, not from humans. No! God does not tempt us to get us to commit sins. Such temptation is against his righteous nature.

There is, however, a way God does tempt us. He allows or creates situations to test our hearts (Deuteronomy 8:2; Proverbs 17:3). Is that what this prayer means? Are we to pray for him not to lead us into a temptation that will test our heart? Again, we answer, "No!" for this is something God purposes for us. God led Jesus into the wilderness to allow him to be tempted by the devil (Mark 1:12-13; Luke 4:1-2). God also leads us into trials to test our hearts to see if we will trust, follow, and obey him as Lord or not. Trials and temptations help us see where we are in our relationship with God. These temptations are designed to make us stronger in character and in faith. Therefore, it is inappropriate to pray for God not to lead us into temptation. He tests our hearts as a test of our faith to see if it is genuine, for such testing is needed and serves a good and productive purpose in our lives (Psalm 26:2; 1 Peter 1:6-7; 4:12-13, 19; Revelation 3:10).

Do we ever fail God's tests that challenge our faithfulness to him and his cause? Do we ever fall into sin? Do we ever suffer bad things happening to us? Yes, we do. Jesus led his disciples to Gethsemane with him when he was preparing for his arrest and crucifixion. His disciples pledged their faithfulness and support, but when the time came, they were not prepared and ran in fear, failing the one they loved and followed. God doesn't take trials away. James, a servant of Christ Jesus, says to count it all joy when we encounter various trials, knowing that the testing of our faith produces endurance. We are to let endurance have its perfect result, to make us complete, lacking in nothing (James 1:2-4). Would we pray for him not to lead us into these things?

Another scripture says that although God allows temptations and tests, he is faithful to provide us with a way of escape (1 Corinthians 10:13). When the disciples' faithfulness to Jesus was tested in the garden during the time of Jesus's arrest, he gave them a way of escape by telling them to pray. But instead of praying like Jesus did and finding God's strength for what was coming, they went to sleep (Luke 22:39-46). When Jesus was tempted by the devil in the wilderness to be unfaithful to God, God gave him scriptures to use to combat the temptations and help him remain faithful to God. One of the best gifts God gives us to motivate us to stay true to him and his righteous ways is the gift of a new heart, a heart that wants to follow Jesus and live as he teaches (Jeremiah 31:31-34; Ezekiel 11:19-20; 36:26-27; 2 Corinthians 3:2-3). To fail God's tests often means we have given in to idolatry (1 Corinthians 10:14). Idolatry means we have looked to something else or someone other than God, including ourselves, to satisfy us and meet our needs.

Since God tempts no one, and since God tests hearts, what, then, can we mean by praying for God not to lead us into temptation? Perhaps what *"Do not lead us into temptation"* means, in light of 1 Corinthians 10:13, is that a good way to practice this prayer is to pray, "Do not lead us into trials that are too hard for us." We ask God to deliver us from the evils of our inner self-centered lusts and wants, from the evils of this world, and from the one who is trying to destroy us.[17] The psalm writer, David, gave us an example of this kind of prayer in Psalm 5. He knows that God takes no pleasure in wickedness and that no evil dwells with God (5:4). So he prays, "Lead me in Your righteousness because of my foes; make Your way straight before me" (5:8). He prays for God's deliverance by praying, "Let all who take refuge in You be glad . . . may You shelter them [and] surround [them] with favor as with a shield" (5:11-12). David gives us a wonderful word in Psalm 9:9-10, encouraging us to trust God as our stronghold.

Jesus twice told his disciples to pray that they would not enter into temptation (Luke 22:40, 46). Prayer for God to deliver us from evil is a very important daily practice. No matter what the Lord teaches us to pray for, whether for daily needs, for God's name to be honored, for his will to be done as described in scripture, for God's forgiveness, or to be protected from evil, the Bible tells us to pray according to the will of God (1 John 5:14-15), in the authority of Jesus Christ (John 14:13-14), persistently and patiently (Luke 18:1), unselfishly (James 4:3), and in faith (James 1:6-7).

"For yours is the kingdom and the power and the glory forever. Amen" (Matthew 6:13). This part of the prayer is not found in the earliest manuscripts of the New Testament. However, it is not a bad ending. It tells us that God has a glorious kingdom in mind, and he has the power to bring it about. In fact, "He rescued us from the domain of darkness, and transferred us to the kingdom of his beloved Son" (Colossians 1:13). We are members of a far better country than the one we currently live in. It is God's country. It is here now and is coming. It is a country that can never be destroyed.

When I was in high school, the athletic coaches would always tell the team when they traveled to games to dress up and be on their best behavior and to remember that they were representing their school. We are from a world that is different from this world. We represent its love and life-giving values to the world around us. Let's show people who we are and what life in that kingdom looks like; they just might want to join us and become part of a good thing. If we mess up and are not the examples God wants us to be, no big

---

17. See F. F. Bruce, *The Hard Sayings of Jesus* (Downers Grove, Il: InterVarsity Press, 1983), 81–85, for a more complete explanation of Matthew 6:13.

deal; we confess it, thank God that he forgives us, pray for his help to do it better, and keep going. Letting outsiders honestly know we have messed up and letting them see how we handle it is also part of what attracts them to God's world.

CONCLUDING THOUGHTS

Questions about prayer trouble many. Some do not pray because they believe it will not do any good. Their experience has been that prayer does not work. Some do not pray because they feel too unworthy for God to accept their prayers. Others think their problems are too trivial and they do not want to bother God with them. Some don't pray because they feel they lack faith, or they fear the pain of disappointment. Because of unanswered prayers, some are angry and see God as uncaring, or they stop believing in God altogether. Maybe all this can change by focusing on what Jesus taught us to pray. We all have our individual ways of relating to God, and he relates to us according to our individual differences. We come to God with many needs and concerns. We pray according to our own personalities. But if we are looking for help and are open to learn and experience the way he taught us to pray, perhaps we would experience more of the results we would like to see, both in us and in our world.

Why is prayer so important to our faith? I am convinced that the greatest object of our faith is the love of God, and the greatest way to grow in the love of God is to commune with him in our hearts. The greatest way we have to commune with him in our hearts is through prayer—that is, being aware of him throughout the day and during quiet times of reflection when we can more intensely focus on him and his love for us. Remembering what he does for us, and has done, lets us know how much he loves us. The greatest thing about prayer is not asking God for things and having him make life turn out as we want. The greatest thing about prayer is drawing close to God and experiencing his love for us.

I believe the greatest object of our faith is the love of God (1 Corinthians 13:13). It is my conviction that the greatest prayer we could pray for others and ourselves is the one the Apostle Paul prayed for the believers in his day. He prayed, "May the Lord direct your hearts into the love of God and into the steadfastness of Christ" (2 Thessalonians 3:5). People say the way to overcome our fears is through faith. Yes, but faith in what? Faith in God's love is the greatest thing to believe in, for experiencing the love of God is what delivers us from all our fears (1 John 4:16-18). Nothing, not even death, can separate us from his love (Romans 8:31-39). The last chapter in this book is on prayer. The last book in this series is on the love of God. I have saved the best for last.

A STUDY GUIDE FOR INDIVIDUALS OR GROUPS

FOR THE LEADER

The following format provides suggestions if you need ideas for leading group discussion. The same format can be used for the preface and each chapter. Some chapters in this book may have questions for study and discussion within the chapter.

Be prepared by reading the material and Bible verses and personally answering some of the discussion and application questions. This helps you add personal input into the discussion.

Choose what questions to ask the group. You may have some of your own.

As followers of Jesus, our relationships need to become deeper than just information sharing. A key purpose of the group is to get to know one another, build deeper friendships, share life stories, and develop loving support by meeting one another's needs. Allow discussion to take its natural course—it is OK to deviate from the script. Decide when to get back on task.

DISCUSSION THAT CAN APPLY TO EACH CHAPTER

1. Consider the title of the chapter. Why would you be interested, or not, in the topic?

2. Read the opening paragraph of the chapter. Share whatever thoughts come to mind.

3. Read each paragraph or section, including the scripture references. Answer any of the following questions:

   - Did anything we just read stand out or seem meaningful to you?

- What is your response to what was just read?

- What point do you think is being made (in the paragraph or Bible verses)?

- How does the verse (or verses) support or not support the point being made?

- Where do you agree or disagree?

- Do you have anything to add to the topic being discussed?

- Are there questions you have that you would like to discuss?

- Can you share any personal stories that came to mind as you read the paragraph or scriptures?

- What have you heard others you know or various media in the world say about this subject?

- Does something said here encourage you, and how?

4. Application questions. Choose whatever ones work for you or your group, or make up your own:

- Did you learn anything new? How was this information a good reminder for you?

- How does this information benefit your life? What would it look like if you practiced this?

- What would you like to do with this information?

- If you want to put something into practice in your life, what is it, and how can others help you?

- Is there any way you can use this information to benefit your family or friends?

- How or when would be a right time to pass on some of these concepts to your kids?

- Is anyone struggling with anything involving this topic? (Be sensitive to each other's needs.)

- Can you share a time when you experienced this or did this in your life? What was the result?

OTHER BOOKS BY JAY R. ASHBAUCHER

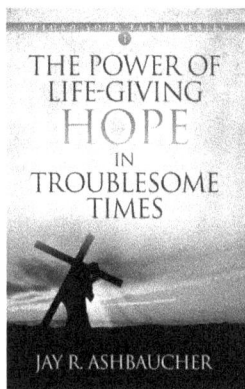

THE POWER OF LIFE-GIVING HOPE IN TROUBLESOME TIMES

Book 1 in the "Upload Your Faith" series

Troublesome times are increasing. Scanning the news and seeing what is happening around the world leaves many with anxieties, fears, and depression. Moral decline, increasing violence, terrorism, and threats of war are everywhere. Americans fear things like a divided country, not having enough money, identity theft, natural disasters, mass shootings, and walking alone at night. Employers complain of difficulty finding reliable workers, and experienced school teachers say it's harder to teach. For Christians, increased persecution is at hand. What's the world coming to? is a common thought in people's minds. Good news! There is hope! This book offers hope and mentions three different kinds. The kind of hope you have makes a difference in the kind of life you live. You can experience a hope that brings joy and peace of mind in the midst of adversity. This book is about knowing the Creator of hope and how this Creator would have us live in times like these. It's about finding life-giving hope that fulfills its promises for a trouble-free world.

OUT OF DARKNESS INTO THE LIGHT: LEARNING TO SEE LIFE FROM GOD'S POINT OF VIEW

Based on Jesus' words that He is *the Light of the world*, this book will help believers better understand their faith and live a richer and more satisfying life. It will assist those who have not yet trusted Jesus to understand what the Christian Way is about so they can come to a more intelligent decision on whether to follow Jesus, or not. The book contains 26 chapters on various subjects to help believers explore and make sense out of everyday questions or issues they may encounter, experience the energy of new life in Christ, and gain hope that sustains them through life's difficulties. To discover Jesus' love, wisdom, and peace is the ultimate aim of the book, but requires that we come out of darkness and into the light.

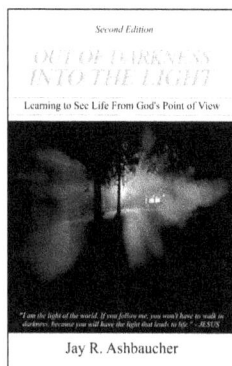

Available now on Amazon.com and other fine resellers.

Author's website: jay ashbaucher.com

www.ingramcontent.com/pod-product-compliance
Lightning Source LLC
Chambersburg PA
CBHW050020100426
42739CB00011B/2722